# THOSE WERE THE DAYS

by
THOMAS CALLAGHAN

Newcastle upon Tyne City Libraries & Arts

TO
**SID CHAPLIN**
A CANNY LAD
(IN REMEMBRANCE)


Also by Thomas Callaghan
*A Lang Way To The Pa'nshop*
*Tramp's Chronicle*

©City of Newcastle upon Tyne, Newcastle Libraries & Arts, Leisure Services
Department, 1992

ISBN 1 85795 005 4

The author wishes to thank Newcastle City Libraries & Arts Local Studies Section and West
Newcastle Local Studies for the provision of illustrations shown in this book. The photograph on
page 18 is reproduced courtesy of the Environmental Services Department, Newcastle upon Tyne,
and those on pages 15 and 121 with kind permission of Terry Quinn. The photographs on pages
75, 100, 130 were provided by Newcastle Chronicle & Journal Ltd. © reserved in all cases.

British Library Cataloguing-in-Publication Data.
A catalogue record for this book is available from the British Library.

# Contents

AUTHOR'S NOTE

Some of these reminiscences have been read by the author on BBC Radio Newcastle. The final part in the book was originally published in the magazine *Iron*.

*Benwell Lane, 1932*

# Preface

These are my reminiscences of the 1930s; an era that was as real and as vital as any other past period in our social history!

My education was quite elementary, my Headmaster a remarkable live-spark. He must have been an astute philosophical sort of man, capable of assessing not only a teacher's merits in the art of instruction but in his or her ability to enforce discipline in the classroom.

There were as many house-traders in those days as there were corner shops! People used their wits in order to supplement their meagre dole money. In my own street alone there was the toffee-cake lady, the ginger beer lady, the ginger cake lady, one lady catering for pies and peas, another who took in washing; and the local fortune-teller lived only a few doors away from the unregistered money-lender. And last but not least, my father was an undercover ragman.

How can I forget the characteristically-named Mrs Rubbing Stone, the odd soul who appeared to be obsessed with scrubbing away at her front doorstep every morning as though she intended eating breakfast off it afterwards! She was the local pawnshop-ticket purchaser, and I was her sole messenger from the age of nine. By the time I was eleven years old she would often invite me into her front room to gaze upon her pawnshop acquisitions; her Aladdin's Cave!

Visiting the public wash-house with my mother, was an education in itself; it was an amazing scene of noise, toil, sweat, gossip, laughter, and pathos.

It was to be a rabbit pie for Christmas Dinner, 1934! There were ten of us in the family, so I appealed to Santa Claus to assist my mother to come across a ten-legged rabbit in one of the butchers' shops on the terrace—no luck—but three of us were invited to a charity breakfast at the local Memorial Church.

When anyone in our permanent state of insolvency had to resort to the services of the local Chimney Sweep, then rest assured it was as the last resort. It was on such an occasion that we came across the remarkable philanthropic sweep; a rare character indeed.

When Mr Cowie, one of my teachers, put my name forward for a week's holiday at Amble, under the Lord Mayor's holiday scheme for poor children, he became my star teacher. Before being awarded this charity plum, the furthest I had been from home was a day at South Shields, another charity trip! A bed to myself, three meals a day, and a sandy beach a few yards away; unheard luxury for all of the kids in the camp.

Who can ever forget the almost romantic figure of the local street Lamplighter! And to witness the Chimney Sweep, and the Blacksmith at work were sights worth seeing.

Jubilee Day 1935! The preparations were almost complete; we were about to begin to celebrate the Jubilee of King George V and Queen Mary! I looked on eagerly, for I was one of the kids present, only too willing to celebrate any event, providing it was carried out by means of eating and drinking, and irrespective of who paid for it.

It was not until I accompanied my father occasionally on his rag trade, that I learned that there could be more to the occupation of ragman, than met the eye; especially so if one canvassed in an area of marked affluence, as did my father! I recall once my father being accosted by a spinster, residing with her father in a big house. She offered my father ten shillings if he would consent to influence her aged father to take a bath; what she really meant was to compel him, without employing force, to have a bath! It turned out to be a battle of wits between my father and the crafty old man.

Sunday morning on the Quayside was the best and the only free open-air show I have ever come across in terms of complete variety. Sword swallowers; Escapologists; Quack Doctors claiming to have the cures for almost every malady except poverty; Racing Tipsters—despite their forlorn appearance they romanced about their supposed connections with Peers of the Realm and other top racing personalities. Indeed, the entertainers were legion.

# School Days

After a spell in the Infants at Canning Street School, just a stone's-throw from the local pit and the quarry, I was transferred to Elswick Road School. On my first day, a Monday, the teacher welcomed me with the words: "Be a good boy, and Jumbo will bring you some sweets," and she pointed to a black ornamental elephant resting on one of the window sills overlooking Elswick Road. When the teacher had directed me to my desk, I sat and pondered how long I was supposed to be good before I received the bribe! It soon transpired that all of us in the classroom were greeted each morning with the self-same words, and that a Friday was the day when Jumbo delivered the sweets. There they were, resting on teacher's desk alongside Jumbo when we returned to the classroom from afternoon playtime in the yard. No doubt the teacher concerned purchased those weekly sweets out of her own pocket. This was a kindly gesture indeed, considering that she could have ensured we were of good behaviour by employing less costly means than fooling us about the supposed powers of Jumbo. However, we were young enough to believe that this inanimate object was able to monitor us during teacher's absence from the room, and even enlighten her on her return as to whether any of us had misbehaved! As I progressed through school I was to learn that it wasn't only in the infants' that children were humoured with such fancies: this inclination continued by means of various instructions throughout the whole period of one's elementary school days; most of what we were taught was unreal and would be valueless in respect of making us fit to combat a harsh competitive world.

By the time I was elevated to the Juniors, I had, besides my numerous pals in Benwell, made new mates in the Bentinck area and in Elswick: like a true comrade I divided my leisure times between all of them. There was Norman Waugh of Matilda Street, Rae Jobling of Bentinck, Albert Ward who lived near the pawnshop at Mill Lane and never once had cause to enter it, the two Holmes brothers, who as orphans lived in the Home next to Elswick Park, and of course Philip Snowdon. He was worth knowing for two reasons: he was clever, and he lived next door to our schoolyard. Many a playtime I was invited over the dividing wall into his yard for a snack of toast or cake and tea.

I was by now attending science class, under the instruction of Miss Watson. She was a firm outdoor type of woman, always dressed in thick tweeds, and strong sensible walking shoes. No make-up ever adorned her plain intelligent face and she wore no jewellery except of course a timepiece on her wrist, which was as large as any pocket watch. Besides other bits of interesting knowledge, she taught us the principles of how to produce distilled water, and unwittingly, in my opinion, how to create various gases! There was very little likelihood of a potential Faraday, Roentgen, Koch, or a Louis Pasteur, rising from this elementary set-up, though once, in the absence of Miss Watson from the laboratory for a few minutes, three of the lads displayed potential as modern-day Guy Fawkeses. They carried out their own experiment, resulting in such a bang that according to the teacher who flew into the room at the moment of impact, the laboratory could have been blown apart and us along with it. I am not sure whether her warning was wise or tactful, given as it was to a room full of young scallywags as we were then. Certainly none of us appeared scared by the event, and the three culprits concerned became heroes for quite some time afterwards, instead of being recognised as delinquents who nearly blew us all to Kingdom-Come! No one was caned on that occasion, simply because Miss Watson could not find out those responsible, and it was more than their life was worth for anyone to be a tell-tale. However, at such a late date, I can say that only Snowdon was clever enough among us to have mathematically engineered such Einsteinian feats in the way of big bangs!

Although she was a pretty tolerant lady, Miss Watson was capable of cracking down on anyone who went out of their way to stretch her endurance. She would use the first thing at hand be it a book, ruler, or her man-sized hand itself, as the means of reprimanding the offender, for she was obviously an advocate of instant punishment. But on the whole there was little need for her to admonish us to any great extent, for she was a very capable lecturer, and most of her lessons were interesting and absorbing. Another important consideration was that in the laboratory we were not having to sit still like over-controlled automata: we were allowed the opportunity of movement from one workbench to another. This fact alone

*Elswick Road School, 1900*

was sufficient to banish the tension and unrest that is created among children who are expected to sit still for abnormally long periods of time when the subject and the instructor are of a boring nature. I loved the practical experiments, especially if they were simple and didn't require any complicated apparatus. A favourite was the generating or making of electric current from, say, rubbing a bar of glass with a silk handkerchief, or a stick of sealing wax treated in the same fashion. This was something I could demonstrate at home to my younger brothers and sisters, to convince them they had a near-genius, or magician, in the family, rather than, as they often thought of me, someone only fit to run messages in search of old bread and bacon-pieces. And of course I was in my glory whenever I had the test-tubes in my hands, placing various measured chemicals into them and heating them over the bunsen-burner, and almost expecting at any moment to discover some potion that would outdo any strange draught that the late Dr Jekyll had invented. It was when Miss Watson lectured on matters that could not be practically demonstrated in the laboratory that my apparent weakness on such scientific subjects as mathematics and logic was sufficient for me to begin entertaining doubts about science. I felt that either I was incapable of following and understanding what she was relating to us, or else—and at the time I considered it a possibility—she was making it all up because she had run out of practical experiments. I was quite prepared to accept her explanations as to the causes of thunder and lightning, and the variations of the English climate; but I drew the line when she related as fact that light travelled about 186,000 miles in a second, and that the earth was 93 million miles from the sun. I thought: how could such impossible knowledge be known to her, or indeed to anyone else? I knew of an intelligent man living in my own street, who, when I inquired of him how many miles it was from Benwell to Heddon-on-the-Wall, hadn't a clue; yet I learned later that it was a mere nine miles away!

My next favourite instruction was woodwork. Here again, as in the laboratory, we were allowed to move around and were kept busy, and when a boy is permitted to exercise both his feet and hands whilst being instructed, few problems arise regarding his conduct. Of course there is always the unfortunate kid who does the wrong thing at the wrong time and gets paid for his troubles, but in both the laboratory and woodwork shop I witnessed far less corporal punishment being served out than was the case in any of the general class rooms. From our woodwork teacher we learned that he had lived for quite some time in the Middle-East, though he never related how he had earned his living out there. One of his most distinctive characteristics was that when, on a rare occasion, his patience with some individual pupil broke down and he resorted to the leather, he would leave the room immediately afterwards, and when he returned appeared deliberately not to wish to cast even a momentary glance towards the offender he had punished; if perchance he did, pain would register upon his face! Apart from his apparent distaste for inflicting pain on any of us, he was a model teacher in all respects.

The very first exercise given to us in the woodwork class was, if I have the name of it correctly, a 'house-joint': two pieces of wood from each of which we had to cut out a section so that they fitted together perfectly in the form of a cross. It may sound to be a simple task but for the majority of us who had previously been unacquainted with any tools whatever except perhaps an axe or hammer it was not so easy an exercise, for the joint hadn't to be a fraction out either way when put together. After a certain incident however I wondered whether the striving for perfection was as necessary as our instructor made it out to be: one unfortunate lad, try as he may, with numerous attempts during many woodwork lessons, just couldn't get his house-joint up to scratch to have it passed. By then the rest of us were progressing on to other practical lessons. Now there is no doubt that nothing is more boring and morale-breaking than being subjected to the same exercise time and time again. One day, whilst the teacher was out of the room, Albert Ward went up to a particular cupboard which as a rule was kept locked, but on this particular occasion the key was still in the lock. He took out one of the house-joint models that had been examined previously and passed by the teacher, and gave it to this lad, taking from him the one he was having no luck with and placing it in the cupboard. At the end of that day's lesson, the lad who had been pretending to have been busy working on his exercise took it to the teacher; and would you believe it, he rejected what had already been passed by himself the week before. Can there be any sense or justice in the world, I wondered!

When we were not being taught how far the earth was from the sun and other aspects of science in the laboratory, and how to carve, chisel and saw in the woodwork class, we were being instructed in elementary arithmetic, in composition, religion, and history. One of the first books on history ever placed in my hands was the work of a scholarly parson, which had been written and published in the early part of the present century. At such an early age I was in no position to question or even ponder how a man of the church, could justify what he described as: the shooting of Red Indians in North America, Negroes and Kaffirs in Africa, and Cannibals in New Zealand, in order that our forefathers could gain a secure foothold in the countries of those aforementioned natives. This man of the cloth also expressed the sentiment that our country must see to it that our boys are provided with rifles and encouraged to practice regularly at the target. Boys' Brigades and Cadet Corps must become the order of the day! I think the poor man got mixed up in his intended vocation. I am convinced that some of the history books given to us to study at school must have been compiled by writers possessing as much imagination as Hans Christian Anderson, or Edgar Allan Poe.

The school bully has always existed. Usually he is on the large size, more brawn than brain, and I venture he will always be around, especially in the private boarding schools; yet the majority of bullies, true to form, are of weak character, and are ready to back down if their well-chosen victim suddenly summons up sufficient courage to retaliate. I think that, during my school days, I was involved in no more than half a dozen encounters of fisticuffs, and every one of them forced upon me by refusing to submit to blustering threats from bully boys. However, there appeared to be an unwritten code, always honoured and always operating during my school days: if a bully was detected tormenting or physically assaulting anyone, a vigilante squad formed instantly and set about him and often enough chased him out of the schoolyard, and thus he had to wait until the bell had sounded and all of us were back inside our classes.

Considering I had breakfast, such as it was, at about eight o'clock on a morning, by the time playtime arrived I was famished. True, I got my free third of a pint of milk, but this only assisted to increase my hunger, not to abate it, and I couldn't expect Philip Snowdon's mother to cater for me too often; indeed, I would practise tact and conceal myself most mornings when I saw him about to climb over the dividing wall into his backyard to enjoy his snack. At such times I would comfort myself by dreaming about the free lunch I would receive at midday. There were quite a number of lads who were sent to school with a mid-morning snack in their pockets, others perhaps with a Mars Bar, or better still something that could be licked for hours, a toffee cake, purchased from a local house-trader in their area!

It was amazing how many unofficial house-traders there were in most working-class districts when I was a lad: enterprising individuals using their initiative to make a small income to help make ends meet, as very few could manage on the meagre dole allowance. In my own street alone, there were three such house-traders. Leaving out the woman who told fortunes, there was the toffee-cake maker, another lady who made the most delicious cakes which no baker in the district could equal, and Mrs Stobbs who lived at the top of the street, facing Broyds the general dealer. Her name to me shall always be synonymous with ginger beer. The first taste of factory-made ginger beer I ever had was a free sample from Mr Reah, who owned the bottling factory at the bottom of the street, and although it was good and I was grateful for getting it for nowt, there was no comparison with the brew of the gods that Mrs Stobbs made in her back kitchen! One could assume that I am accustomed to exaggerate the particular qualities of certain individuals, but rest assured, I only sing the praises of anyone or anything after careful consideration and stringent comparisons.

The question of our long summer school holidays was seldom a problem for the mothers in my neighbourhood, especially for those of us receiving free school dinners, for they continued during the holidays. Then in the afternoon all we required was half a stotty-cake with jam inside it, and a penny if our mothers could spare it, and off we went to the park, and never returned before bedtime. There were no bored-stiff kids around then, for when a child has to more or less create its own pastimes, then experience through the ages shows that the child's imagination seldom lets it down; its own make-belief world is its Shangri-La, which it will cling to most determinedly.

One Monday morning during the summer holidays, I arrived in the next lane to my own to call upon a pal of mine. I found quite a commotion going on between two women who shared the same backyard:

"You know bloody well it's washday, an' you using the wash-house for that kind of goings on; who do you think you are?"

It soon became evident to me that one of the women had discovered the other drowning four newly-born kittens in the wash-house boiler, and on a Monday of all days. But I was puzzled as to why the debate had overspilled into the lane when the issue in hand had arisen in the wash-house in their own backyard, and where the dispute ought to have been settled. I could only assume both of them were exhibitionists and so enamoured with their respective powers of rhetoric, that they wished to captivate an audience with it. I observed that the husbands of the women were standing together silently at the back door, wisely remaining neutral:

"Well I've told you once already, I can't afford to feed five cats, can I?" responded the other woman.

"Good enough Bella, but you could have used the bloody bucket to get rid of them. An' another thing, I think you ought to keep an eye on that cat of yours, it's always havin' kittens."

Even when the dispute fizzled out and they returned indoors, I still remained uncertain as to whether the argument had really been over the morals of drowning kittens (no matter what receptacle was employed to do it in) or over the unhygienic use of the backyard boiler; whichever was the case, one thing was certain: the feline population of Benwell had decreased that morning, at least by a total of four.

When I entered the backyard of my pal, I discovered the wash-house boiler fire was lit and the basket of washing in the yard. His mother was undoubtedly preparing for the weekly wash. Their scullery door was wide open yet not a sound was coming from inside the house. I knocked, then entered, as was the usual arrangement whenever I called upon this particular mate of mine. His younger brother and baby sister were sitting on the mat amusing themselves with a toy fort and soldiers. My pal, Alick, at that moment came out of the front room, which was his mother's bedroom. I had observed it was in darkness, the curtains being closed, and I sensed at once that the poor soul was obviously suffering from one of her periodic migraine attacks. The father of the house had about deserted his wife and family, despite his occasional visits, and my pal (who like myself was only ten years old) had decided that the best way to lessen his mother's burdens was to act as a father-figure to his brother and sister, and with some success: hence their remaining silent, having being told by him that their mother was unwell. He asked me to assist him in bringing back the laundry basket from the yard, realising his mother would be in no fit state to tackle the chore at least until the following day. But on the spur of the moment, and being fully acquainted with my own mother's washing-day routine, having assisted her a number of times, I suggested to Alick that we do the washing ourselves so his mother could take it easy for a couple of days. He took a little persuading but finally agreed! Now those old fashioned poss-tubs and poss-sticks were huge objects in days of yore: the poss-sticks would have made formidable clubs for any strong-arm assailant, but the weight of them was no problem; I felt myself equal in strength in that respect. The difficulty for me was that the poss-tub was too large and too deep for me to cope with the possing effectively without some means of a platform to stand upon. I experimented with standing on a chair but I nearly fell head first into the poss-tub. Next, I secured roller skates on to my shoes, but I kept gliding away from the tub, struggling to keep my balance as though I were a drunken ballet dancer. Finally, with an old pram, I made a trip on to the terrace where the Sutton Dwelling housing estate was being erected, and so waiting my chance I borrowed a number of building bricks. These made an

*Possing the clothes*

ideal platform and so we got on with the work. By the day's end, we knew
how it felt to poss, scrub and mangle a whole week's laundry in one session.
Having the backyard to ourselves, as the people upstairs were at Tynemouth
for the day, we decided to hang up all the washing on the lines in the yard,
instead of placing it out in the backlane and perhaps providing gossip for the
neighbours—though I assure you, the washing was a real treat to look at. No
Chinese laundry could have done those sheets and towels and the other bits
and pieces that go to make up a complete family wash any better than we
had, and without the aid of today's modern magic soap-powders all of
which are supposed to wash whiter than white. All this work-energy had
been provided solely by two-penneth of chips and bread and marge between
four of us: naturally the toddlers had to be fed, after all they had been
fighting imaginary battles with their toy soldiers all day long without a
murmur. No parent could have been prouder than was my pal of those two

youngsters for keeping out of our way time we did the laundry, 1934 style!

Now I can understand children being interested and attracted by the sight of a wedding going on, for it is usually a colourful and gay affair; but I couldn't understand then what fascinated some children (and I was one of them) in the solemn spectacle of a funeral! The first funeral of the day, not unlike weddings I suppose, has to commence early on a morning if the vicar concerned has a full day's programme ahead of him, for in all decency that very reverend gentleman has to spend a reasonable time over each event. Therefore it was not uncommon on reaching the cemetery gates on the way to school to be held up by a funeral procession slowly making its way into the cemetery. In the days I write of, it was still customary to take one's leave of the deceased in a slow dignified manner, with many of the mourners walking behind the carriage which was conveying the relations. During the time I attended Elswick Road School, I reckon I was late but twice, and on each occasion it was owing to a sudden decision to discreetly follow a funeral procession down to the graveside to observe the last rites; and each time I was accompanied by a number of lads all from other classes than my own. The ways of children are odd indeed!

The fortune-teller who lived in our street had a fair reputation. She was known to be pretty good with the cards, and the tea-leaves in one's teacup. She was always having visitors, some of whom came from outside the district. There was another couple living in the house, relations I believe, and they had a young son; both of us often played at cowboys in the yard, sometimes in the house if it was raining. Therefore, on the occasions when she had a visitor in the front room, we would sit in the hallway ever so quiet and fascinated because we were able to distinguish every word she was telling her client about their future, or relating to them a message from some departed husband or other deceased person, for the lady concerned was very versatile. She was able to switch from fortune-telling to being an intermediary between her clients and the spirits without any problem. The majority of her visitors were females, mainly middle-aged. Only twice in a number of years did I ever witness a gentleman client call on her. I remember one early evening, sitting in the hallway outside the front room door, hearing her remark to a client that there was going to be a disaster for someone in the neighbourhood in the near future. Within two weeks of that date I was entering the street one morning on my way to the baker's when I observed three fire engines at the bottom of the street. On investigation I discovered that the bottling factory was almost gutted. From that moment on, I held this lady fortune-teller in complete awe. So did her husband, but not for quite the same reason; indeed, he looked upon her private activities as a kind of joke, an opinion which of course he kept to himself, but I knew, for he had expressed his feelings on the matter numerous times in my presence. The reason he held his wife in awe was that being unemployed, like most of the other men in the area, and realising that his missus was making a little money at her crystal-gazing profession, he was dependent on her for the bit of pocket money that came his way, and he had to humour her. The odd thing about this most harmless man was his habit of forever dosing himself with bicarbonate of soda. I sincerely believe his obvious addiction to this salt assisted in his demise before his time. If ever he was to run out of this product and didn't have a copper to purchase another packet, his misery was such that it soon affected the whole household, and someone would eventually tip up, despite probably being aware he was scaling the lining from his stomach with the compound.

I think my love for the countryside was born during the first Blackberry Week's holiday that I spent in the way it ought to be spent: by going abroad and picking berries from the hedgerows. From the Monday to the Friday, after completing my morning's delivery of newspapers, I set out with one of my many pals, and discovered cornfields, green pastures, woods, country lanes and hamlets, and neat little railway stations adorned with colourful flowers and other plants. On the Monday I set off with Gerry, who lived in my backlane, each of us equipped with our bait, a bottle of water and a large tin for the berries. Up Ellesmere Road we went, and on to the West Road, over a field which took us towards Cowgate Co-op dairy, past Buist's garage, and at once we were in the countryside, with farmland on either side of the road. Opposite the old Kenton Bar stood the small Post Office-cum-tuck shop, and a few yards further on we were into Kenton Woods! One swift exploration convinced us that the fruit bushes were saturated with large juicy blackberries, so we decided to sit down in this leafy paradise and eat our bait at once for we didn't have to worry where the next grub session would come from. Afterwards we began picking, but no sooner had we filled our tins with berries than we sat down again and ate the lot. How we never suffered from the cramp, only our stomachs could have told us, but they were apparently willing to accommodate all that we could send down to them. It surprised us that no one else was in the woods gathering the fruit harvest, not that we were unhappy with the fact. The only company we came across in the first couple of hours were the birds and the countless rabbits. There were so many rabbits about, and all of them apparently so trustful of us, I reckon we could have returned home with at least half a dozen each, had either of us been capable of wishing to kill such playful creatures, for they seemed intent on pushing their luck and were almost running over our feet.

*The old Post Office, Kenton Bar, c1935*

Finally, with our tins and stomachs loaded with fruit, we left the woods, made our way down the lane and on to the perimeter of the farm, arriving at another old pub called the Runnymede. From there we walked down Stamfordham Road and followed the tramlines up to Fenham Hall Drive, being surrounded by farmland all the way. I don't think either of us had ever spent such an interesting time in our lives, and without the cost of even a

*Fenham Hall Drive, c1935*

halfpenny, not that we had one to spend. Next morning, after delivering my papers, then selling firewood (all in aid of helping to make ends meet) I again set off with Gerry and we made our way to Westerhope. We commenced our search down a country lane opposite the Runnymede pub, and the bramble hedges were thickly adorned with fruit. In the afternoon we came across a number of miners on their way home from Walbottle colliery who were also picking berries using their work helmets to house them:

"Well yeh bugger, nee wonder we can't find any ripe berries, these two nippers have picked the lot," remarked one of them in a jovial manner.

I peered in turn into his helmet, and observed the berries in it were as black as any one of their faces: "Yeh have your share, Mister, there's not a red berry to be seen in your helmet."

However, I proposed to him to give me a penny for my lot knowing full well I would be able to fill my tin again before I packed up for the day. He offered me a halfpenny.

"Do you think I'm daft, Mister, just 'cause I'm small?" I retorted, being determined not to entertain any bargaining, as though I was a cheapjack stall-holder in a Persian market. "It took me two hours to pick these, and I know a woman in wor street who makes cakes and tarts, and she will give me tuppence for these," and I made to walk on:

"Ah'll give yeh a penny for them nipper," called out one of his mates. "Stingy Ned here, he would rob his mother to save a halfpenny." But the other miner chuckled good humouredly as he pointed a finger towards his critic:

"Nipper, divint be fooled by Davy there; he'll flog them same blackberries to his next-door neighbour for tuppence. Davy does nowt for nowt."

And indeed, Davy burst out laughing, and despite his black face I could detect that he had blushed, which led me to believe he had purchased my berries with the aim to self-profit. And good luck to him, thought I.

On the Wednesday I set off once more, this time in the company of Alick Kirkwood, the lad I had assisted with the laundry. Over Geordie-Goddard's field we went, past the offices of the Board of Guardians, a building which had once been a private residence in its own pleasant grounds. I brought Alick's attention to it:

"That's where the people gan who want a food-ticket from the Parish when they've had their dole stopped. But they've got to make sure they haven't anything to sell, like a piano or gramophone, 'cause they send a visitor to spy on you first!"

Within minutes of crossing the West Road we were on Cowgate Moor and passing the Castle Hills, from whose summit one could see clearly as far as New Bridge Street in the City. We began picking the berries in the narrow country lane leading towards Kenton Village. By the time we arrived in the village our tins were nearly full, so considering we only had bread and margarine for our bait, we sat down outside the blacksmith's shop and got cracking on the bread and fruit, after first giving the smith a large handful:

"You'll both get the tummy ache eating that lot in one go," he called out as he fed his own face:

"We won't Mister, both of us have had plenty of practice. Does the horse eat blackberries, Mister?" I asked, as he began filing away at the horse's hoof:

"I don't think so nipper," he replied, "but I do." I took the hint and gave him another handful before moving off.

Next to the smithy, was an old chapel and nearby was a large pleasant looking farm house belonging to the Younger family. By the side of the house was a farm track and we decided to follow its course. This brought us to the village of Fawdon. Changing our direction westward we followed the rail track along to Kenton Bank, picking and eating berries all the while. Most kids are blessed with elastic stomachs. Finally, we ended up by the Jingling Gate pub in Westerhope! By the time Friday afternoon arrived, I had travelled for miles around the western suburbs of Newcastle, picking blackberries. Most of the territory we covered consisted of farmland, a few small hamlets, miles of railway tracks and small pretty railway stations! Today, all those idyllic scenes have vanished; only the memory of them remains.

*The Jingling Gate and smithy, Westerhope*

As we moved house from Benwell to Elswick, my brothers and sisters and myself were transferred to South Benwell School. I was still in the juniors for another year. My teacher was Miss Nash, a young smart looking lady; and for the first time I really began looking forward to attending school, despite the nonsense being ladled out to us under the guise of education. When a pretty girl, called Anne, was placed next to me at my desk, it took all my powers to resist dividing the secret affection I held for my teacher with Anne, though I managed the effort! By a coincidence, my elevation to the seniors, situated at the top of the old Victorian building, marked the departure of Miss Nash, who left to get married. But she returned later, as Mrs Bell, and in time she became headmistress.

Early morning began in the assembly hall; though often enough in these old-type schools this large space was, after assembly, converted to perhaps two or even three classrooms by means of sliding-partition screens. On the first morning in the seniors we were greeted by Mr Anderson, the headmaster, who stood up on a small stage next to the piano. He was a medium sized, ruddy complexioned, bespectacled gent, and he soon left us in no doubt about what he expected from all of us new recruits: punctuality and obedience; discipline was his speciality! Then he paused in his remarks, peering down upon us rather wistfully as though expecting, even hoping, that one of us would give him some sign, or display some form of dissent, but there were no takers. By this period in my life, and mostly due to my vast experience of meeting various types of people on my paper round and firewood business (besides being local messenger-boy for a number of neighbours) I was becoming accomplished in determining people's characters, and so from the beginning of my brief observation of the head teacher, I sensed he would be a live spark at the drop of a hat. After introducing himself he stepped down, and Mr Dixon, a rugged-faced ginger haired teacher, who also wore spectacles, began conducting the morning songs of praise as he played the piano. He appeared to have a passion for music and for singing, and expected everyone to share his strong feelings.

We were soon to learn that it was not only the headmaster who was a stickler for instant obedience. His staff, huge physically-fit specimens, were only too keen to show any offender what they meant by discipline. If the hapless victim were perchance to be a boy who was mortally afraid of his father at home, then rest assured he would be ten times more frightened out of his wits by the time any of these disciplinarians had finished with him. Whenever the headmaster was chastising any boy, the spittle shot out as though it were jets of acid. He appeared to be about to lose control of himself.

It was after a little while in the seniors, that I first witnessed the headmaster get to grips with an offender. We were returning from playtime in the yard and were all in the corridor each of us making towards our respective classrooms, when this lad, for what reason I know not, grabbed hold of another boy, punched him and began using his victim's head as though it were a conker-nut. Unfortunately for the aggressor, he had banged the lad's head against the headmaster's office door. It opened instantly. It was obvious he must have been behind it, poised for any sign of trouble at such times. His keen critical eyes took the situation in at a glance, and as the aggressor released his hold on his victim, the headmaster grabbed hold of him with one hand and with the other pushed the lad's chin back so that his head was pressed against the wall, meanwhile calling out: "What are you? A duck egg, duck egg, duckie-duckie..."

The more angry he grew, the more inarticulate he became, and so he frog-marched the culprit into his office for the sake of privacy, and no doubt to give himself time to cool off!

However, I must add that the headmaster was often a most genial man when his humour was in good fettle and there was nothing around to upset his equanimity; as in most instances with individuals who are apparently blessed with a touch of brimstone in their make-up, he could be unpredictable when one least expected it. One day Mr Dixon had cause to leave the classroom for a little while, and so Mr Cowie next door left both his classroom door open and ours, assuring us of what the consequences would be if anyone created a disturbance. After a few minutes' complete silence, despite most of us having ceased our studies, I moved towards the teacher's desk, not without a little encouragement of course from the rest of the lads, climbed upon his high stool and began a mock history lecture. This created mirth to the extent that I only sensed I had close company when sudden silence stole over the room once more. To my horror I realised the headmaster was standing beside me. After a brief warning to the rest of the class, he told me to follow him to his office!

"Close the door, Callaghan," said he, going to his desk while I shivered in my old sandshoes. To my surprise, and relief, he brought out of his desk drawer not his leather strap, but a mint which he stripped of its wrapper and placed in his mouth. He peered at me quizzically over his spectacles across the width of his desk for a few seconds before speaking further: "Fancy yourself as a historian do you?" he asked, the shadow of a smile upon his lips. I shook my head to indicate that I held no such views about myself, but he, like my father, wanted nothing to do with such horse-like gestures. "Speak up laddie. You were managing alright in the classroom," said he a little impatiently at my employing nods of the head in place of articulation:

"No sir. I was only telling them about Robin Hood, to keep them quiet," said I, still full of trepidation.

"Well, you weren't being very successful in that direction," said he, continuing to peer at me intently. "I hear you have a paper-round, is that correct?"

"Yes sir. The blacksmith on the quarry told me it would help me mother to make ends meet," I replied. He smiled briefly:

"You're a bit young for delivering papers; however it won't do you any harm, and it will help your mother. Now then, go back to your classroom, and not another peep out of you do you understand?"

"Yes Sir," I said eagerly, amazed at not being punished as I had expected! From that day onwards my opinion of him changed for the better.

Mr Cowie, over six foot tall and with the build of an athlete, was the teacher who in addition to his normal duties, was the physical training instructor, whether in the playground or on the football field. Like most children, I loved any form of exercise that allowed me to escape the precincts of the school for a couple of hours or so, and I looked forward to our weekly visit to the recreation ground on Condercum Road. From the first afternoon of my appearance on the football pitch, it became obvious to Mr Cowie and his assistant that I would never be of any value to any football team. The truth was that I did not have it in me to take any field sport seriously. My leisure time, away from selling and delivering newspapers and hawking firewood, was spent on the quarry playing at cowboys. However, I was soon to discover that I was far from being alone in the respect of being thought hopeless at football, rugby or cricket; there were very few possible star turns among us. The most capable lad I witnessed performing on the field was Billie Donaldson, who eventually was to play for Newcastle United. Despite my failings as a footballer or cricketer, the opportunity to play solely for pleasure and not as a challenge, was sufficient joy for me, and to be outside in the fresh air was the best part of the whole exercise.

It was on those rare school outings, such as a trip to the Hancock Museum, that I formed the opinion that it was possible to learn more of value then, than was possible in the classroom. Even our visit to the Cremona Toffee Works on Chillingham Road was of far more value educationally than reading about some industrial enterprise in the classroom. All of us were fascinated to be in the presence of working men and women operating such amazing machinery, and to have our demanding questions answered. This was real exploration of the industrial scene. Another worthwhile visit was to the offices of the *Newcastle Evening Chronicle* on Westgate Road to witness the paper being printed. I considered this event a special occasion for me, for I was, indirectly, one of their employees. I had been selling that paper since I was eight years old! These visits to industrial premises, museums and art galleries were in my opinion too infrequent and ought to have been increased in number, for their educational value for most children is immense. Witnessing and experiencing the real world around us would have been more beneficial than some of the classroom instruction which was delivered and which most of us for various reasons never absorbed, or even understood. It takes a whole lot of training and practical experience, and a fair command of good diction as well as being able to elucidate clearly, to become a good teacher.

When Mr Cowie put my name forward for a week's holiday at Amble, on the Northumberland Coast, under the Lord Mayor's holiday scheme for poor children, he forthwith became my star teacher. Before being awarded this charity plum the furthest I had been from home was a day in South Shields, another charity hand-out. Never before had I been away from home overnight, let alone a whole week. As soon as I arrived in Amble, and was billeted in the large communal hut, I volunteered and was accepted as batman to Mr Cowie who was lodged in a cubicle at one end of the hut. Every morning after breakfast before going down onto the beach, I swept his room out and made his bed, polished his shoes, and tactfully concealed the beer bottles that were lying around. Never in all my young days was I so keen to rise on a morning, despite having at my disposal the unheard luxury for anyone in my social circumstances, a bed all to myself; not a second longer would I linger after hearing the first musical notes of *Stars and Stripes Forever* over the camp relay-system. I was determined to be one of the first in the washroom, and afterwards one of the first in the dining room. I couldn't somehow get over the fact of being sat down to a breakfast of porridge, bacon and egg, bread and butter and marmalade, and as much tea as one's drainage system could cope with. Before coming to Amble, I didn't think it could be possible that I would be able to leave the table feeling content and satisfied. If only poor Oliver Twist could have sampled fare as I did then, I feel confident he would not have run away from the Workhouse and landed up in the cesspools of London.

In the Camp was a large cinema-concert hall where some evenings we were entertained by a film show, but on our last night there was a two-hour concert show, and the range of talent among the lads from the backstreets of Tyneside was amazing. There were good singers, tap-dancers, comedians, acrobatic wizards, and one individual who displayed an astonishing memory by rendering without a pause the dramatic and many versed *Legend of Dan McGraw*. This Lord Mayor's holiday camp concert was performed with practically no rehearsals whatever, yet the quality of much of the show would not have shamed the stage of any variety hall!

Mr Smart, another robust character, was the art instructor. Like the other teachers, he was a firm disciplinarian, but he always remained in control of his emotions. He never exhibited any signs of a temper that was liable to erupt, yet all of us felt he would brook no opposition to his instructions. One of his joys in life (apart from art) was rugby, the game he had once played.

The male teachers especially, at my school, were weather-beaten captains who were capable of sailing their educational craft and controlling their elementary crew. Mutiny was unheard of and the few hard cases among the pupils reserved their rebellious moods for the backlanes. I was never once caned by Mr Anderson, the headmaster. That alone amazes me even now. Nor did I ever feel the leather from Mr Smart. I received my share of punishment from Mr Dixon, often I didn't know why, nor I suppose did he. Mr Cowie made me twinge a few times, and the other teachers gave me my share of the leather. However, I always forgave my tormentors. I realised they didn't mean it, and I suppose there is nothing more trying in this world than being the keeper of a roomful of young demons.

# Mrs Rubbing-Stone

In my childhood days in Benwell, it was a custom for everyone to take turns in cleaning each other's front step, and such tasks were religiously carried out daily. However I knew of one lady, whom I had always identified in my mind as 'Mrs Rubbing-Stone' solely because she used more of that name sake commodity than any other woman in the district, and she was the only exception as far as the sharing out of this particular chore was concerned. Indeed, as far as I could ever ascertain, her upstairs neighbour never got the opportunity to take her turn, for Mrs Rubbing-Stone, like the proverbial early bird, always beat her to it, and no doubt in time the lady upstairs accepted the situation in good grace, and who wouldn't?

I first observed this keen early morning step-scrubber when I was eight years old. I was on my way to the nearby local bakery in quest of old bread. There she was, on her knees scrubbing away at her front doorstep and putting as much effort into the task as though she intended partaking of breakfast on it afterwards. On my return from Jennings' bakery about ten minutes later, she was busy giving the same meticulous treatment to her upstairs neighbour's step. I stood a few seconds to admire her applying of the elbow grease, and she must have taken umbrage at my sudden interest, for she brought the rubbing-stone to a halt, glanced up at me, and inquired a trifle haughtily: "Have you got nothing better to do than stand and watch me, laddie?"

Having been taught never to cross words with my elders, I uttered not a word, but continued on my way home. Mind you, her abrupt attitude didn't disturb me any. On the contrary, I was well used to that kind of treatment from certain grown-ups; so the following morning and every morning afterwards, I bid her good morning, and in time she responded likewise. But our relationship speedily developed on a particular Saturday morning when she accosted me as I was on my way down to the terrace to shop around for bacon-pieces, and she asked me to bring her a rubbing-stone from Storey's, the hardware shop: "Now this is the colour I want," said she in a determined manner and holding up the stone she was using at that moment. "You know what colour this is don't you?" she asked decisively.

"It's the colour of ginger-bread, Missus," I responded. She smiled, looking pleased at my appropriate description:

"That's right laddie, so don't let him give you any other colour. Some of those shopkeepers will sell you anything if they can get away with it!"

I had by then formed the opinion that such was her zeal and no doubt her energy, spent towards the upkeep of those two front steps, that if given the opportunity she would have volunteered to scrub and apply her favourite colour of rubbing-stone to every other doorstep in the street whose colour did not comply with her own.

It was when I began trekking to the fish and chip shop late at night, hoping for larger servings at such a late hour, that I discovered another peculiarity of hers: the cleaning of the inside of her front room window most nights, and this task oddly enough was always performed with the room in darkness. In time I became convinced that her window cleaning activities were a blind; what she was really after was to keep tabs on the few individuals staggering up the street from the terrace, where they had been spending perhaps those sums that ought to have gone to the rent collector or ticket man. I was of the opinion she had a pecuniary interest in the social misdemeanours of such mortals, for Mrs Rubbing-Stone, was a pawnshop-ticket purchaser, and I was to learn that this expensive habit of hers had resulted in her becoming a hoarder of other people's pledges!

My reputation as a regular pawnshop visitor soon reached her ears, and so I was engaged by her on a permanent basis. I don't think that Mrs Rubbing-Stone, had ever pledged anything in her life, further, she didn't like visiting them. As far as pawnshops were concerned she was by nature, and no doubt by means, a redemptor. As a collector of other people's property she could aptly be described as a human magpie. On one particular occasion when she approached me to pay a visit to the pawnshop to redeem an article, she cautioned me most carefully: "Now be careful how you carry it lad, it's a clock you're going for!"

To me, the warning was quite unnecessary, for being accustomed to shopping for cracked-eggs, which I always returned home without ever having a mishap, carrying a clock would present no problem. On my way and following what was my usual custom, I acquainted myself with the details on the pawnshop ticket, and to my amazement, I learned that the clock I was redeeming for her was our own; and of course I had had the task of pawning it. This little incident alone convinced me that Mrs Rubbing-Stone was yet another character, from the many in the neighbourhood who employed me as a messenger-boy, who looked upon me as being thick-skinned and without feelings. Each time I returned from one of these redeeming missions, she would take the parcel from me and present me with a penny, never would she ask me into the house. However, by the time I was eleven years old, she began to take quite an interest in me, whether on account of my business efficiency, or with her having no children of her own, I could not assess. But one Saturday morning on my return from the pawnshop she invited me into her front room! I looked on in amazement at the results of my many trips to the pledge shop. The contents in the room reminded me of an Aladdin's Cave. What attracted my particular fancy was what appeared to be a beautifully coloured miniature peacock in a glass case resting on the chest of drawers next to our clock. There were other clocks, all shapes and sizes, on the mantleshelf, pictures on the walls, vases and antiques on other shelves, drawers full of silks and Irish linen, an expensive-looking silver teapot; the list was endless! I often pondered on what her aims were in redeeming what were in effect other people's treasures and basic necessities, which due to hardship they themselves could not afford to recover. Were they intended as some form of security for her old age, as Fagin himself confessed to Oliver Twist on Oliver's discovering the miser gloating over his loot? Or were she and Fagin on a par, in the respect that they hoarded such dispossessions solely for the pleasure of them? Certainly, Mrs Rubbing-Stone had invited me into her sitting room deliberately to show off her pawnshop acquisitions.

There was no doubt in my mind that Mrs Rubbing-Stone possessed an artistic temperament in relation to her favourite chore, for no woman devoid of it could have devoted as much loving attention as she did to those doorsteps, and her front window sill. The way she would back away from her window sill to admire her handiwork reminded one of an artist withdrawing a little from her easel to appreciate the almost completed work; then she would move forward again with the rubbing-stone in hand to apply another dab here, a touch there, until finally she was satisfied with the results!

I suppose the continuous scrubbing of any material is bound in the long run to produce effects other than the desired results. Certainly stone steps are not immune from wear and tear, no matter how much rubbing-stone is applied after the scrubbing; and Mrs Rubbing-Stone, an eccentric character if ever there was one, was far too heavy in the use of the scrubbing brush to be doing those two steps any good. I could, without a doubt, observe that the depth of those two steps she so diligently scrubbed were diminishing year by year. One morning I felt compelled to remark: "Don't you think you're wearin' those steps away, Missus, scrubbin' them so much?"

Now whether the rubbing-stone slipped involuntary from her hands into the bucket of water at my unexpected intervention, or whether she had allowed it to fall into the bucket deliberately due to exasperation at my innocent observation I could not honestly say, but she raised her head promptly and peered at me with an ill-tempered scowl upon her face and retorted: "Don't you think you're wearing your tongue out talking such nonsense laddie? Don't you know that what the scrubbing brush takes off, the rubbing-stone puts back on! Goodness knows what they teach you at school these days."

From that day on, I never passed any further critical remarks on Mrs Rubbing-Stone's odd behaviour; certainly not in her presence!

# The Public Wash-House

When I was a boy, all the domestic chores in my neighbourhood were done by hand: dough kneaded for bread-making, floors scrubbed, the front step lovingly dressed with one's own favourite colour of rubbing-stone, windows cleaned, and of course the family laundry possed and ironed! Monday, as far as my neighbourhood was concerned, was universal washday. So on a Saturday or Sunday, depending on the weather, I would leave home with my empty poke, and scavenge round the local quarry in search of firewood, and the local pit heap for slag-coal. The competition for such necessary commodities to cope with the combustible appetite of the backyard wash-house boiler was very brisk for those of us existing on the economic prudence of the Means-Test brigade.

I had just returned from my early morning paper round and was sitting down to my breakfast, such as it was, when my father addressed me:

"Listen Son. I want you to stay away from school today and give your mother a hand to the wash-house, and also keep an eye on your sister. I've got to go out tatting, to see whether I can earn a few coppers."

"Yes, Dad" I replied, not liking the idea but too wise by then to display any dissent.

It was a Tuesday, raining, and had been doing so for the past two days, so unable to put off the washing any longer, my mother had decided to go to the public wash-house in Bond Street. After breakfast we filled the large wicker-work laundry basket and set off. At the top of the street my mother sent me into the corner shop for a half pound of Sunlight Soap, or if that was unavailable to get carbolic. I suggested Fairy Soap, thinking if it was good enough for the Little People to use, it ought to be good value, but she thought otherwise: preference habits are hard to break, I suppose. I was wearing an old jacket of my father's, which naturally was large enough for my young sister Mary to shelter under, though it hindered me a little because of having to assist in carrying the large cumbersome laundry basket. After my mother had paid the admission fee at the office, we entered the wash-house:

"Hello, Carrie. Long time since you've been here, hinny," called out one of the women in greeting my mother. "I see you've got a good strong looking assistant with you," she added, referring to myself, as we set down the basket at one of the vacant wash-boilers.

*The public wash-house: Gibson Street Baths (New Bridge Street) c1908*

Placing her coat and hat into the now empty laundry basket, and securing a large piece of sacking round her waist, my mother began her Herculean task. My sister and I sat down in a corner near the entrance, and I was soon enraptured with the factory-like scene before us: groups of women stood in three rows, scrubbing, or possing, rinsing or mangling. Of course there were the inevitable few who appeared to have come solely to gossip and critically scrutinize those whose laundry was the worse for wear. The almost feverish activity of the scrubbers, the poss-stick thumpers, and the manglers, soon had the floor around them covered in puddles of water. Those fortunate enough, to have clogs on their feet, like the staff present, and those women with a good pair of solid pit boots on (no doubt their husband's) could afford to be indifferent to the numerous pools of water on the floor. But for those like my mother, wearing well-worn shoes reinforced with cardboard soles, their feet would be saturated within minutes of starting work, and apart from their immediate discomfort, many of them could end up with a shocking cold as their reward for doing a hard day's graft.

"Sally. Did your Nellie get that job in the Grainger Market?" called out a woman who was busy scrubbing a shirt on the bench.

"Yes she did Maggie. But we're no bloody better off, 'cause the Means-Test people have cut-doon my man's dole money on account of it. Wor Nellie's fuming, she's talkin' about leavin' home an' goin' into a furnished room."

"Proper home-breakers, that's what the Means-Test people are," interjected a small woman, wearing a large man's cap and oversized wellingtons on her feet. "If I were you Sally, I would write a letter straight away to the Prince of Wales. He'll liven the buggers up; he knas what the poor people have to put up with, God bless him!"

"What's his address, Lizzie? I have a few complaints to bring to his notice," called out Maggie.

The little woman wearing the big cap, although apparently detecting the tone of mockery in the remark, nonetheless replied quite placidly: "If you write to him c/o Buckingham Palace, London, that ought to reach him Maggie."

"When you do write to him Maggie, ask him if he has a spare room to let for our Nellie," quipped Sally, shaking with laughter.

By now, as more women got busy on the wash boilers, the ever-rising steam had the place as uncomfortable as a Turkish bath establishment, yet only one of the women had the nerve to disrobe down to her slip: a fine-looking figure she had too. The frocks that the majority of the women were wearing were as thick and as cumbersome as the heavy outdoor coats they had arrived in. They would be exhausted before they left the wash-house. I thought to myself that had it not been for the question of drying the clothes my mother would have been far better off washing in the backyard wash-house despite the rain. And I could have been at school into the bargain to receive my free midday lunch of perhaps shepherd's pie, and spotty-dick pudding smothered with custard. I had heard tell, previous to this, my first visit to this sweat-shop, that the doing of one's laundry was far easier and done more efficiently at the public wash-house than in one's own backyard. This was not my opinion even though many of the women in the wash-house assisted each other in the more arduous tasks like mangling.

"Are you havin' a Jubilee Party in your lane next year, Lizzie?" called out Sally.

"We will be if I have anything to do with it. Twenty-five years they've been on the Throne, God bless them!" replied the little woman in the big cap, who then glanced defiantly over in Maggie's direction, as though expecting a critical retort from that quarter, on account of her avowed respect for the Royal Family.

But Maggie appeared to be holding a close and serious whispered conversation with one of the obvious gossipers. I began listening carefully to the discussion taking place between Sally and Lizzie, on the possible holding of back lane parties in the May of the following year, 1935, to celebrate the Jubilee of King George V, and Queen Mary. Personally, I was only too willing at that age to support and celebrate any event, providing it was carried out by means of eating and drinking, and irrespective of who paid for it.

At that moment a woman and a young girl entered the wash-house, carrying between them a large tin bath containing an immense amount of laundry. I had thought that our own washing load, for ten of us, would have taken some beating, but their lot was huge, and the tin bath created for me the impression of being a gigantic pot-pie all ready for some field kitchen. It was no wonder the pair of them had arrived so highly coloured and almost gasping for breath. After unloading the washing into the boiler, the woman ordered her daughter to hurry back home with the tin bath, as by now, she reminded the girl, her father would be home from the pit, and would want a bath before going to bed: "Pick it up, girl, it won't bite you," roared out the impatient woman to her daughter, who was no taller or older than myself, and certainly not as strong.

If the woman had been blessed with only a fraction of common sense, she would have realised that irrespective of it now being empty, the tin bath was far too large and cumbersome for such a wisp of a girl: "Come on, pick it up girl, your Dad can't wait all day for you. He must have his bath before he goes to bed," remonstrated the woman, even though as yet the poor girl had not uttered one single word. Try as she might, she was unable to hold the tin bath and when she made to trail it along the floor, this was met by a fresh inconsiderate outburst. Suddenly all of the other women ceased working, and observed the young girl struggling unevenly with the large tin bath. Despite the continous sound of the laundry machinery and the hissing of the steam, I felt as though the wash-house had become enveloped in complete silence, and the atmosphere was almost electrically charged. I began to wonder who among the washer-women was going to take up the cudgel on behalf of the girl, and chastise her mother. My bet was either on Sally or Maggie, both massively-built creatures. But it was neither; it was Lizzie, the little woman:

"What can you be thinking of, hinny? Expecting a bairn, to carry that whopping big thing on her own, God bless her!"

"My man's got to have his bath when he comes from the pit," bawled out the impatient woman, whose temper was now becoming very frayed: "Do you expect my man to come here for it?"

"He's welcome here for a bath in one of the poss-tubs, there's plenty of hot water, and anyone of us will scrub his back for him," called out an anonymous voice from behind some machine.

The laughter resulting from this sally did nothing to pacify the tin bath woman, and for a brief moment I thought she was about to give vent to her feelings by pouncing on her uneasy-looking daughter, and thrashing her, but she somehow appeared to overcome the impulse. At that moment, my mother beckoned me over to her side:

"Give the girl a help home with the bath, son, to please me."

Turning to my young sister, I told her not to move while I was away, then offered my services, which were accepted rather reluctantly by the woman concerned!

Of all the quaint errands I had done up to the age of ten, I considered helping to carry a large tin bath through the streets was the daftest, and I was more than pleased that it was raining heavily so there were not too many inquisitive folks about to stare or perhaps enquire where we were off to with a tin bath in such weather. Fortunately the girl did not live too far from the wash-house. When we entered her backyard her father was standing at the scullery door seemingly awaiting her arrival. Dressed in dark trousers, nondescript shirt, black face, neck arms and hands, he looked like

Al Jolson, waiting in the wings for his cue to prance on stage and begin singing *Mammy*. The instant he spoke, I judged his temperament to be quite the reverse of his wife's; he sounded genial and affectionate, and I observed the girl was at ease in his presence. He greeted me with a broad smile which displayed his teeth, looking so white in contrast to to his coal black face:

"Wat-cheer, marra! Doing your good deed for the day, hinny?"

"Yes Mister," I replied, feeling at ease in his company.

"That's the stuff t'give them nipper. Bring it in and place it on the mat before the fire the pair of you."

And we followed him into the the parlour, placing the bath down in front of the roaring big fire. Immediately the fat ginger cat who had been basking on the brass fender jumped into it and stretched itself full out, yawning in the process.

"Hey there, ginger-chops, I'm having me bath before you have a kip in there," remarked the miner to the cat.

As I made to depart, he caught my arm gently, and beckoned to one of the chairs at the table:

"What's your hurry man? Sit doon awhile and let's hear your crack! I'll bet you're playing the wag from school, like my Nancy here, and helping your mother with the washing. Am I reet or not?"

I reckoned it was a fair conjecture on his part to assume I had met his daughter in the wash-house, and I nodded my head in confirmation. Nancy brought out his breakfast from the oven and placed it on the table in front of him: there were about six or seven links of sausages on the plate plus an egg and the lot surrounded by tinned tomatoes. I thought to myself: he must work hard down the pit, but by jove he gets well fed for his troubles; and I would only be too willing to work alongside him and his mates, to be served with such large helpings of appetizing grub. The girl cut him two thick slices of bread from the large home-made loaf and buttered them for him, which was as well for he tucked in to his meal without even bothering to wash his hands. By now the kettle on the hob was whistling as though reminding the girl he had a date with a nearby teapot. Once the tea was brewed she filled up her father's pint pot, and was about to sit down when he reminded her of my presence:

"Come on me little flower, pour your help-mate a cup of tea out, and cut him two slices of bread and I'll put a couple of sausages on them."

With the thick sandwich on a plate and a cup of tea before me, I was now prepared to forget my absence from school and the loss of my free midday lunch! Well just about, for suddenly I thought of my sister back at the wash-house. She too would be hungry, so I discreetly asked the girl for a paper bag to place half of the sandwich in.

"What you going to work at when you leave school, marra?" he inquired, having by now disposed of his breakfast.

"I might be a blacksmith, or a singer," I replied without hesitation.

He placed his pot on the table and peered at me more inquisitively. He could not have appeared more surprised had I expressed the intention of taking up some unusual occupation such as a stunt-man, or lion-tamer. He glanced over to his daughter and both of them began smiling quietly as though sharing some secret or private joke:

"Singer, me lad!" he gave a chuckle. "Well I never, would you believe it, that's another one for the book." And he pointed over to Nancy who by now was giggling away merrily: "That makes two of you wanting to be singers. My girl, there, she wants t'sing with a dance band on Radio Luxembourg. I don't know where you kids get all those funny ideas from. I think you better settle for being a blacksmith, and come doon the pit and tend to the ponies, you'll be sure of a regular wage packet that way. Well I never, singers!"

I observed the cat had dozed off, no doubt due to the excessive heat being thrown out from the huge fire which reminded me of a blacksmith's forge going full blast.

"I had better get back to the wash-house, Mister, me mother might be finished her washing," said I, rising from the table, and the girl rose too.

"Well marra, it's been nice listening to your crack; any time you're passing this way just look in and let me know how your going on."

The pair of us left the house and made our way back to Bond Street.

"He's a good man is your dad," said I to the girl, "but I wouldn't like to work doon the pit and get as black as he does. When I leave school I think I'll be a blacksmith, but not doon the pit like your dad says. If the pit ponies ever want new shoes from me, they'll have to come to the surface for them 'cause no blacksmith can work in the dark!"

"My two brothers are going to go down the pit when they leave school, and so would I, if I was a boy," said she determinedly.

"What do you want to work doon the pit for?" I asked, rather surprised by

*Benwell Colliery, Charlotte Pit, c1900*

her admission.

"Because you get a load of coal delivered to your house, and for nowt," she replied, looking askance at me with a rather bemused countenance, as though bewildered at my apparent ignorance.

"My dad says no working man gets owt for nowt off the gaffers, so your dad, cannot be getting his coal for nowt," I replied.

That ended all conversation between us, for I rather think she gave me up as being hopeless, apart from assisting to carry empty tin baths, in the rain, to the amusement of every passer-by.

My mother was busy giving the final rinse to her washing when we arrived back. I sat down beside my sister and gave her the sausage sandwich:

"When will it be time to go home?" she asked, sounding bored, having by now exhausted all her curiosity as far as the wash-house activities were concerned.

"It won't be long now pet, just eat your sandwich, then go to sleep if you want to."

Meanwhile, Nancy was being directed by her mother to go down on to the terrace to do some shopping. As she left the wash-house, a tall lad aged about fifteen entered. He was wearing a raincoat and old trilby. He began peering around and finally caught sight of Maggie:

"Mother, are yeh finished yet? I'll niver find work if I have to keep commin' t' this place, an' runnin' messages all day lang."

"Have you got the bogie with you son?" his mother replied, completely ignoring his complaining attitude.

"It's ootside in the rain. I think me father should come an' give yeh a hand, he niver does owt," went on the lad, continuing to grumble.

"Your dad's out looking for work. You know that," replied his mother, deliberately glancing around her, as though she was relating the last piece of information for the benefit of the other women rather than her son. But her action was a wasted effort for he instantly let the cat out of the bag:

"I knar where he is, in his usual haunt in the public library readin' room gapin' at all the newspapers; an' yeh can tell him that, if yeh want to."

"No. You tell him son, when he comes in for his tea," remarked his mother, still sounding placid enough.

"I'm not afraid of me dad. There now. Have yeh finished the washin' yet?"

"Just a few more minutes. I'm going to start filling the basket now, son, then you can hurry home on your own," replied Maggie.

"You should never complain about helping your mother, son," chipped in Lizzie. "She's the best friend you've got in this world and the best you're likely to get."

The tall lad looked towards Lizzie, critically surveying her big cap and oversized wellingtons, before deciding to reply:

"It's alreet talkin' like that, Missus, but I won't find work hangin' around these wash-houses will I?"

"Work is hard to find these days, son. We're living in hard times. The Prince of Wales knows that, God bless him," replied Lizzie.

"What's he got t'dee with it?" retorted the lad caustically, before walking swiftly away towards his mother as though intent on getting away from Lizzie's presence.

Maggie, having neatly folded the last sheet with the assistance of Sally, placed it into her large laundry basket and her son picked it up, refusing any help from his mother. As they came towards the exit his mother beckoned in my direction and addressed her son:

"There's a lad who helps his mother willingly without complaining." He glanced down on me in his dry manner:

"What's he got t'complain aboot, he's havin' a day off school isn't he? You wouldn't let me have a day off school when I was goin'."

When they had departed, the tin bath woman commented, to no-one in particular: "If he was my laddie, I would clout his ears until they were as hot as my kitchen fire!"

And I thought to myself: by jove, the lad's ears would be hot, if they reached the temperature of that kitchen fire of hers. One thing was certain, there would be no danger of her husband, the cheerful miner, catching a cold whilst bathing in front of that conflagration.

Although like my mother, I was blessed with great patience, having in life been conditioned to that virtue, I was nonetheless pleased to observe her filling up the basket with the completed laundry, and I wakened my sister who had by then dozed off.

I only wished I had been old enough and strong enough to have carried the basket on my own, for I saw that my mother was very tired. And a limited breakfast of bread and margarine and tea, was no support to begin a job that would exhaust even a navvy.

# The Quarry

For many families, the Sunday lunch was one of the highlights of the week, possibly the only day when they could afford a joint, and the only day of the week when the favourite Yorkshire Pudding was included on the menu. Once the dinner was in the oven, the mothers would begin baking, for no Sunday tea-time was worth sitting down to unless the table was spread with such mouth-watering treats as apple or rhubarb tart, scones and stotty-cakes! Whenever my own mother couldn't afford such a spread, then I hoped one of my more fortunate pals would get his mother to invite me to tea.

Now unless a husband was a useful and willing help around the house on a Sunday, most women wanted rid of their menfolk when they were so busy:

"Why don't you walk over to the quarry and get out of my way for a few hours!"

The Quarry was situated behind the Grand Cinema, and rest assured the more unwilling home-helpers would require no further encouragement:

"Ah well, lass, I might as well gan and have a game of quoits with the lads."

"That's reet hinny. But keep out of those gambling schools, do you hear me?" A depressed sigh, before the obvious retort:

"I've got nowt have I? So I can't play."

Part of the quarry was taken up with allotments, and the maze of alleyways that led to-and-fro was ideal for the lads playing at Cowboys and Indians. Also these lanes afforded concealed havens for the three-card brag schools. The only snag for the card-players was when the pitch-and-toss schools (which on account of the nature of their game required ample open space) were being raided by Police. Naturally those being pursued, being fully acquainted with the layout of the alleyways, which led up to a newly constructed housing estate, ran off in those directions. Pity those who may have been sitting concealed in those lanes playing cards, for only the swiftest of the three-card brag players would have had any chance of escaping the law, once they had been bowled-over by a frantic pitch-and-toss runner!

I learned from an early age that all these clandestine gambling schools had strict rules.

Rule 1: they didn't allow children to be present in a group. This was not, I suppose, for fear of corrupting their young minds, but rather for their own safety, for if the gamblers had to vacate their pitch in a hurry, they didn't wish to have an extra encumbrance to deal with on fleeing the scene. Mind you, they had no objections to having one eagle-eyed, fast-sprinting kid around (me), to act as a look-out.

Rule 2: if any player lost his total capital, he was out of the game post-haste (no credit allowed). However, if any individual player wished to loan the insolvent a sum to carry on playing, this was alright, providing all the other participants agreed to it.

Rule 3: anyone who was winning a fair amount could not drop out of the game of his own free will, he had to wait until the morning or the afternoon session came to an end. The penalty for one who was foolhardy enough to attempt to ignore this rule was that he must be prepared there and then to expect to visit his panel-doctor next morning, or at least the butcher to purchase a beef-steak to ease the swelling that would have developed by then around the vicinity of his peepers.

Rule 4: don't be caught cheating, as the penalty for this weakness was the same as for Rule 3!

A Sunday on the quarry was usually a lively time for me, for apart from following my own boyish activities playing at cowboys, I was at liberty to wander round from one gambling school to another, amusing myself at the almost eccentric antics taking place, so long as I kept moving and didn't get in anyone's way especially that of a loser's. Sometimes I would be employed as a scout, therefore my presence was on an official footing. As a scout, my tactics were to slide down the banks of the quarry on some tin-sheet every ten minutes or so and give a glance along the terrace in both directions. If any Policeman happened to spot me, well with the tin-sheet in my hands, he would see how I was passing my time away, therefore I could continue to observe him innocently and ensure he was not intending to pay a visit to the quarry. If he was, then I ran up the bank and gave my warning whistle, and as a lad I could whistle some.

The only two games I ever witnessed being played in the quarry by adults, but which did not seem to attract the close attention of the law, even during the process of a raid, were marbles and quoits. Money changed hands nonetheless. I think the safeguard was the fact that these games were always played without any money being on show; winnings were discreetly passed over after each successive game.

*Benwell Quarry c1900*

I well remember one particular Sunday morning. I was idling my time away observing a game of quoits being played by a group of local miners, and I was offered the task of returning the thrown quoits to the players. Being always eager to earn a penny, I welcomed the offer! The game of quoits goes something like the following: the players stand about 18 yards from the hob (a thick iron pin which is secured into the ground). If the quoit thrown rings the hob, the score is two, and any quoit falling near to the hob scores one. The quoit is about eight inches across, and concerning its weight, well, sufficient to say that if the quoit thrown was by some misadventure to miss the hob and come into contact with someone's head instead, then it is a fair bet that the one who stopped the heavy metal ring with his cranium would soon have the undertaker attending his remains, and the player who threw the quoit would soon be attending a Coroner's Court!

Within minutes of taking up this Charles Atlas exercise, I was regretting, for the first time ever, volunteering to earn a penny. For a penny I would be able to purchase a lucky bag in the baker's shop on the terrace, but what I would find in the bag would in no way compensate for the calories I was burning up in stooping to lift those heavy disks. What was required for such employment (for by then I refused to look upon this pastime as sport) were the large servings of leek-pudding and mince-and-dumplings which I felt sure these miners would be accustomed to, but which I unfortunately was not. So I took it upon myself to bring my lunch hour two hours forward. I didn't get my penny but neither did I continue to risk being exhausted for the rest of the day.

One Sunday morning about ten-thirty I was passing by the Bond Street Memorial Chapel, when I was joined in company by Ginger, an acquaintance of mine. Ginger was four years older than myself, and by build alone he appeared like a burly blacksmith. His huge hands, which I observed at that moment were freshly bruised, no navvy would have been ashamed to own. He brought from his jacket pocket three packets of Beech Nut chewing gum and handed them to me:

"Keep your jaws busy Tommy."

I knew then, by instinct, that he must have been using some local chewing-gum vending machine as a punch-bag:

"Where are you off to, Ginger?" I inquired, after thanking him for the gum.

"The same place as ye, I think, the Quarry!"

Now this lad, although only fourteen years old at the time in question, was the only kid in Benwell who was allowed to participate in the gambling schools in the quarry: he was the youngest adult around. He smoked, gambled and was able to use his fists with the best of the scrappers. Now if we had, by chance, met the local Policeman as we progressed towards the quarry, then no matter in what direction he may have been going at the time, or which side of the road he was on, the Bobby would have paused and begun to feign an interest in some object in a shop window, his sole intention to observe whether Ginger was heading for the quarry. If he was, then the Bobby would realise that gambling was expected to take place there. But Ginger would be aware of the Policeman's interest in him, and he would cross the road, go down Atkinson Road, and once out of sight enter the cemetery to scan the terrace, and, if all was clear, cross over the road and on to the quarry.

One of the pitch-and-toss schools was already in progress when we arrived:

"Have you seen the Bobby on your travels Ginger?" called out one of the players.

"Na. He'll be in his Police Box beside the Adelaide Cinema, havin' his tea break at this time in the mornin'."

Ginger's word was good enough for them, for they well knew he kept a wary eye open for any signs of the law, and as a result it was commonly believed that he was fully acquainted with the daily movements of every Policeman on the Benwell beat at any given time. I'll wager he wished he had been: it would have made life for Ginger that much easier.

One of the onlookers took two pennies from his waistcoat pocket, spat on them as a gesture of good luck and challenged Ginger to a flutter:

"What do yeh say, Ginger: am I on, two heads for a tanner bet?"

"Alreet. But nee barrin' them. Divvent touch the buggers till they hit the ground," replied he without hesitation.

"There's nee danger in that with me, laddie. Once I toss them up I let them take their own course, yee kna that," said the miner, placing the coins in the palm of his hand.

With a flick of the wrist he sent them up spinning. They landed at odds, one heads, one tails. So he gave them a second spin with the same results, then finally they landed tails upward, and Ginger pocketed his winnings:

"Want another bet?" asked Ginger.

"I'm skint, you've took me last," replied the miner, appearing dejected.

"What! Comin' here with a clarty tanner in your pocket," remarked Ginger.

"Lend's a tanner till t'morrow?" asked the loser seeking possibly the means to recoup his loss.

"Bugger off kidder, an' gan to your allotment an' feed your leeks," said Ginger.

"There's nee need t'be cheeky aboot it," retorted the miner. But Ginger had already forgotten his presence and was interesting himself in the main game taking place, obviously seeking the first chance to join it.

Big Harry was holding court in the centre of the main game, surrounded by punters and spectators; and all of them would have dearly loved to skin him, to make up for all the times he had cleaned them out! Big Harry was a miner. He was also well over six-foot tall without his pit boots on. I had often pondered why such a big man as himself had decided to work down the mines, especially considering he was a face-worker, and at times, according to his own testimony well supported by other pitmen, he had to graft in seams of only two-foot or even less. Even with him lying flat on his belly or his back, this would still leave very little space for such a big man as he was in which to engage in coal-cutting. I felt sure there must have been times when he was at work that he wished he was about two-foot tall. Quite a character was Harry. If ever there were such a breed as the big spenders, or, more correctly, big gamblers, then Big Harry, taking into consideration his limited means as a working man, belonged to those ranks. Spinning coins up into the air for single bets of a half-crown, was commonplace to him. If anyone was as simple as to mention pitching bets to the value of a clarty penny, and no doubt they would have to be strangers to the school, he would either ignore them, or verbally obliterate them, depending on what mood he was in at that particular moment. Harry liked the straight dollar bets, but his real preference was for currency notes to be changing hands, from theirs to his! As could be expected, he held Ginger in great regard. Both of them were gamblers by nature, if that is possible, but despite their addiction to the excitement of the game they never lost sight of the main purpose of it which was to win, though, like all natural gamblers, they remained unruffled whenever they lost.

Not many of the three-card brag schools were keen for the company of Big Harry, or Ginger for that matter. Without doubt Harry was the most notorious advocate of blind-brag in the area. Most of the card players didn't mind one or two rounds of blind-brag but the majority of them, being cautious by nature or means, were soon lifting up their cards to see whether they had a good enough hand to continue betting. The odd one might attempt a little bluffing on perhaps a Jack-high, but in the face of determined opponents, they soon packed in. The frustration really began when perhaps only three players were left in a game and two of them continued to bet blindly, and of course the stakes were rising every turn round. Big Harry, or Ginger, were the ones to test the nerves of most of the card players in this respect, and more than often the one with the best hand threw his cards down, unwilling to risk his lot against the blind-braggers. In time, Big Harry and Ginger were only admitted into a card game on condition that blind-brag would just be allowed for a few rounds in each game!

Neither in the three-card brag game, nor in the pitch-and-toss school could one claim that skill was necessary; you were either lucky or you lost. However there were individual players in both schools who disputed such a clear analysis; for instance there were card players who swore that a particular pack of grubby looking cards brought them luck. Others claimed that a particular mascot such as a rabbit's foot, or some other meaningless object which they never came out of the house without, brought them luck. There were players of pitch-and-toss who would no more enter a game without their favourite two pennies, than would some bowl players play without their woods. Ginger was about the only gambler who remained unimpressed with such fads, and he was the luckiest player among the lot of them!

Big Harry was becoming a little impatient. Apparently there were no big spenders in the game currently taking place. A few of the men were willing to accommodate Harry on a couple of half-crown bets, but no higher. They obviously wished to spin out what money they could afford—or rather ill-afford—for as long as possible, at least until twelve o'clock opening-time on the terrace. However, I had often witnessed a number of them lose what coppers they had put aside for their Sunday pre-lunch drink, and have to go home and slake their thirst on home-made ginger beer, unless one of the winners invited them to a couple of pints.

Big Harry broke away from the main game on seeing Ginger, and no one dared complain, even though he had been one of the winners.

"Hello Ginger. Are you game for a dollar bet?" asked Harry.

"Alright. Toss the buggers up soon as you like," replied Ginger.

It took three spins before the toss declared a winner, and Ginger was five shillings richer.

"Double or quits: what do you say Ginger?" said Harry as he brought out a ten-shilling note from his back trouser pocket.

"That suits me," replied Ginger, remaining cool as ever. "An' I'll stick to tails, if you divint mind."

The other players from the main game, the small stake merchants, ceased spinning their own coins and began joining the already eager throng of spectators around Harry and Ginger. Two tails again! And Ginger held out his hand for the note.

"By Jove you're a lucky sod," remarked Harry, still holding on to the ten-shilling note. "Want your chance doubling it again, marra?"

"Yes Harry" replied Ginger. "But let's feel that ten-bob note for a while if you divint mind, 'cause I've a feelin' it's niver gan to change han's again." And he grinned good naturedly.

Big Harry smiled: "Don't you be too sure laddie, you're the first one I've lost to this morning."

"An' I'll be the last," quipped Ginger as he prepared to spin the coins.

"He wants taakin' doon to size if you ask me oot," remarked one of the onlookers, in an undertone, to the man next to him on his right.

"He's not a bad sort," replied the other man. "I'll tell you one thing, he niver sees anyone beat for a smoke, and he always seems to have tabs on him. He's a funny bugger on the quiet."

"Ah divint knar aboot that," retorted the first man. "I still divint think it's reet, a kid of his age, gambling an' smoking; an' as far as I hear, he can drink his fare share of Broon Ale. I'm sure he niver went to school either."

"He can still read and write mate," said the other man decisively. "And they divint teach them more than that at school, least not in the ordinary schools."

If such an event had ever occurred before I certainly had never witnessed it nor heard tell of it! I had of course witnessed Big Harry lose his lot, with the exception of his mid-day beer money which he always kept separate from his gambling funds, but as the nearby Parish Church clock struck twelve noon, Harry was cleaned out in every sense of the word, beer money, the lot, with the exception of his favourite two pennies which he always held on to. Mind you it hadn't been a completely one-way affair. At one time during the game, Ginger had been down to his last five shillings, then luck once more took over. I agreed with the final majority opinion that it had been Ginger's morning from the beginning and that the session could not have ended any other way than it did. It was quite a spectacle, as the clock ceased chiming, to witness Ginger, the fourteen year old dead-end kid, offering the big man who was over thirty years old, a loan until his next pay day, and Harry accepting willingly.

Not all of the local miners spent their Sunday leisure hours at pitching pennies, or quoits, or at cards, indeed not all of them could afford to do so. With regard to those who were unemployed, they were always the spectators of such games. Among those who were out of work there were those who, as miners, couldn't find a job in any of the numerous pits in the district. The simple fact was that not all the coal being mined could be sold. The unemployed were in no position to purchase much of it. Some couldn't afford any and relied upon searching the pit-heaps. Those miners who didn't gamble, for whatever reason, spent their leisure time in various other pursuits. Some played endless games of marbles for the fun of it; others kept racing pigeons. Once a group of these bird fanciers got together on the quarry, where their lofts were situated, then the banter that was sure to follow was worth listening to:

"Your pigeons can what, Fred? Fly from Benwell to Durham in under an hour? My birds could walk it in that time. It's time you started feeding the poor buggers on corn instead of weeds," remarked one of these individuals in my hearing one Sunday morning.

"I divint doubt aboot your pigeons Joe. They would have to walk it, they haven't the strength to fly," retorted Fred.

"Listen to these two comics, Davie, talkin' aboot pigeons," remarked a bantam-sized character, to another of the company. "The pair of them haven't a bird in their lofts that could find its way over the road to the cemetery and back."

"Now careful, Willie," responded Fred, "I've told you before, any of my pigeons are big enough to carry you on their back and take you to Chester-le-Street, where you belang, you little foreigner."

Benny, another miner, had one of the most interesting hobbies a man could ever wish to follow, if he had the inclination for it, that of wood-carving! The first Sunday morning I ever introduced myself into his company, he was sitting outside the locked-up blacksmith's shop, not far from the pitch-and-toss school. I soon became fascinated, and pondered how such large knarled hands could perform such delicate and neat workmanship. I also discovered that morning that he did not take too kindly to people standing over him while he was working:

"Sit doon nipper, if you're intending to stay awhile."

And as directed I sat down between him and his pal. Ever after that, having first satisfied myself that I was not required to act as a scout for the gamblers, and after having engaged in a little eavesdropping on the pigeon-fanciers, I always joined the company of Benny and Matty, and was greeted more in the manner of a confederate than just a curious-minded lad. They never had any occasion to change their mode of conversation on my arrival, for neither of them indulged in language that could be termed vulgar. I never learned whether Matty had any hobbies, and I never witnessed him gambling. Chewing baccy, plus long-range spitting, and a good natter, appeared to be his ideals for passing the time away. The range of topics between these two men was pretty wide: they discussed their work in the mine, trade unions, politics, and often they would take a trip down memory-lane, reminiscing about their childhoods in Benwell. Although, like most kids, I was inquisitive, and ever ready to shower anyone with questions on lots of subjects if I got the opportunity, I was tactful enough not to invite myself into their conversation, and this factor, I believe, was why they never objected to my joining their company! I well remember one of their political discussions, which I believe went as follows: Benny happened to remark that in his opinion the Socialists were akin to Christ. Matty appeared, for an instant, to have swallowed his cud of baccy:

"I think it's blasphemy, talkin' like that, on a Sunday. Benny, hinny, you ought to be ashamed of yourself. You mean you would associate the politics of people like Ramsay MacDonald, and Snowdon, with the teachings of Christ? Gaffers' men, serpents, men who betray their own class, men who Churchill praises and looks upon as comrades..."

"Now hold on, Matty, son, hold on!" interrupted Benny. "Get on the right track will you? In the first place, neither Ramsay MacDonald nor Snowdon belong to the working class; they're members of the bourgeoisie, like Churchill. I was referring to Socialists! People like Keir Hardy, and Willie Gallagher. They preach the teachings of Christ. They do in my opinion. Accuse me of blasphemy if you like, I don't mind."

But whatever the topic taking place between them, it never halted the activity of Benny's hands for long, they seemed to itch for the wanting to carve some wonderful effect, whether it be that of some whimsical-looking human, or animal head-piece on the top of a walking stick. Benny had never had an art lesson in his life, yet he was none the worse for his lack of training.

On account of living in overcrowded conditions and with the back lanes as my nearest playground, I envied those lads whose fathers had an allotment. Fortunately, being pals with a couple of these kids, I was able to visit their gardens and sometimes give a hand. Then after a couple of hours of pleasurable weeding, we would be hailed up to the cabin for tea and cake. At such moments my pal and I would pretend we were cowboys having our chow in camp, and food and drink never tasted better than under such conditions. What a pride these allotment-holders took in their cultivation of flowers and vegetables, especially the leeks, which were displayed in the club before ending up in the broth pan or leek pudding. Then of course with the majority of them being unemployed—as far as wage earning went—they had all the time in the world at their disposal to nurse their crops. These men were not only an asset to themselves and their families, but also to the local community, for they constantly patrolled the terrace and the streets with their bogies collecting the horse-droppings for manure. Often on a summer Sunday afternoon, the whole family would retire from the back lane to the allotment in order to to take advantage of the sunshine and the long light evenings, not always to labour but to laze around for a few hours. Mam and Dad would sit on the garden bench and perhaps enjoy a natter with the neighbours on either side of their own garden while the kids studied the progress of the caterpillars and other garden insects. About seven o'clock a slow stroll home, kids off to bed, dad reads his paper, mam has a nap. End of a perfect day, without the cost of a penny.

# Going Tatting

"How can I go tatting without the price of a packet of Woodbines in my pocket?" urged my father to my mother, on one particular morning in 1934. "I've got something arranged today, that's why I'm keeping Tom away from school."

My mother stood with her back to the fireplace keeping her eyes fixed on my young sister who was sitting on the double bed in our living room:

"You told me yesterday you would make a few coppers in High Heaton which is one of your favourite rounds, but you didn't earn a penny, hinny," said she, anxiously fingering her purse inside her pinafore pocket. "I've only got one shilling and fivepence to last until you get your dole on Friday, and I don't know what we'll do tomorrow if..."

"What you worrying about woman?" interrupted my father. "There's bread and marge and vegetables in the house, and the kids get their dinner at school. I've been promised the remnants of a jumble sale this morning and your sister, Dolly, will buy that lot. Then I intend going tatting as well. You know I wouldn't keep the kid away from school for nothing."

My mother withdrew her purse and extracted two pennies from it. My father spat on them for luck before placing them into his waistcoat pocket. After he had kissed my young sister, he told me to get a move on, as I was struggling to tie my shoe lace.

"Me shoe lace is not big enough, Dad," I remarked. He bent down, and instructed me how to solve that difficulty:

"Just miss a couple of lace-holes like this, right! For goodness sake try and use a little imagination," said he, still sounding irritable after the Woodbine debate.

Placing the sack which he used for tatting inside a carrier-bag, we set off for the Labour Exchange on Scotswood Road. It was a Wednesday, one of his signing-on days. When we arrived at the dole office, the busy scene reminded me of the Vickers Armstrong factory round about lunchtime: men and women coming and going out of the building in a continuous stream. The main difference here of course, was that the majority of the unemployed faces wore a mask of total dejection. Some of the men who had already signed the register began idly chatting to others who were outside waiting their turns to go in. I observed that at one of the windows of the Police Station which was on the opposite side of the road, next to the wash-house, two Officers were peering out, apparently giving their attention to the loiterers. I formed the opinion that both buildings were ideally situated in relation to one another, indeed they couldn't have been better planned. Any individual feeling he possessed the right qualifications for the Force had only to cross the road and voluntarily enter the main entrance of the Station to chance his luck of being accepted and so escape from the bread-line brigade. On the other hand, any individual in the dole office who suddenly gave vent to his feelings of frustration over his benefit claim, and attempted to take it out on one of the clerks, would soon find himself being involuntarily led into the main entrance under the 'Blue-lamp'! I suppose as things were, from an economical point of view, a month's free board and lodging in Durham Gaol was something to be considered, at least as far as a single man was concerned and having no one to worry about time he was inside.

"Here son, put this carrier bag under your arm and wait outside for me," said my father, nodding awhile to a couple of signing-on acquaintances. I stood with my back to the Exchange windows.

I knew there were no vacancies being advertised in them so I wouldn't be in anyone's way. I couldn't avoid overhearing the discussions going on among the various groups, not that I wished to. One small group were discussing the state of the nation, and whether any public money ought to be spent on the Royal Jubilee celebrations the following year; a second group were debating about grub, and the lack of it, whilst a third gathering were verbally lashing some individual jockeys, describing them as 'toe-rags', on account of letting them down on the racecourse the previous day. One of the loungers recklessly brought out a packet of five Woodbines, lit one, and put the packet away without even appearing to apologise for his indifference to the nicotine-starved men around him. Some of them ceased chatting momentarily on whatever subject was holding sway at that time and eyed him up eagerly; one or two of them glanced at him rather maliciously and moved away from him as though the temptation to throttle him might become overpowering if they remained too close.

When my father came out of the dole office, he indicated his intention of calling upon my Aunt Dolly, whose secondhand clothing shop was along the road in the direction of the cattle market.

"Hello Jimmy, Hello Thomas," greeted my Aunt, as we entered the shop.

My father, not a one to waste time on discussing anything but the business in hand, told her of the jumble sale remnants he expected to collect from the church hall on Sandyford Road, and asked whether she would be interested. She told him what would be particularly useful, then gave him a shilling before we left. On arriving at Gallowgate, to my surprise and delight, my father took me into the café situated a few yards from the wholesale rag and scrap merchants, and he ordered two teas and a slice of bread and dripping for me. All of the customers present appeared to be rag merchants, and my father was known to them all. One of them came and joined us at our table:

"I'm glad I've seen you Jimmy," said he, addressing my father in almost a whisper. I couldn't grasp the whole of the remarks, but I did learn that he urged my father to go to a certain bakery on City Road at three-thirty in the afternoon, for by that time a certain exhibition of bread-making that was taking place would be over, and the bread was to be distributed to any unemployed men on production of their dole cards:

"Don't forget Jimmy, be there by the time I've mentioned, and whatever you do, don't let on what I've told you. There will most likely be enough of us in the know without broadcasting it."

"By God, Joe, I'll be there alright, and I know how to keep my tongue still, and thanks to you," replied my father.

"This dole business is getting me down," remarked a man sitting at one of the other tables to his company, though talking loud enough for everyone in the café to hear him. "I'm sure our lass thinks it's my fault that I'm unemployed, the silly bitch that she is. And her mother is another one. The pair of them are always picking on me and I don't get a meal in peace. As regarding her mother: Bottle and Jug Lil I call her. She's never out of the local snug. I think it's her who stirs our lass up, I would be better off joining the Foreign Legion."

"Why don't you volunteer for a six months stretch at one of those labour camps that the Ministry of Labour are running?" asked one of the men at his table. This apparently innocent inquiry almost created a right rumpus.

"You call them labour camps, mister?" called out someone from a far table near the counter.

"You believe that men go willingly to those bloody places?" shouted another man from the same table.

"Let me tell you, Bill, what my view is," remarked a man from the table where my father and I were sitting. "They're prison camps, that's what they are. The only buggers who ever volunteer to go to them are the staff. Anyone else has no option, you either go when you're told, or else get your dole stopped. If I were you, Bill, I would read what Wally Hannington has to say about the Ministry of Labour camps."

"I was only joking, yeh knar," remarked the man who had inadvertently set off the heated debate.

"Come on son, it's time we got moving," said my father to me.

Before we left the café, my father and his pal informed each other discreetly in what area they were intending to canvass for rags and scrap. They always made it a rule to work within calling distance of one another so if perchance one of them was lucky enough to score for a fair haul, they could call upon the other to assist, and share the proceeds.

On hiring our barrow from the dealer situated next door to the wholesale scrap merchants, we cut up by St James' Boxing Stadium then down into Percy Street, at which junction my father told me to climb up on to the handcart. We had just turned into Sandyford Road, beside the Barras Bridge Hotel, when my father was accosted by a well-dressed eccentric-looking gentleman with a camera in one hand and in the other a leash which was secured to the collar of a dog. Attached to the dog's collar was a luggage label:

"Excuse me, my good man," said he. "Is the Barras Bridge Post Office far from here?" My father rested the barrow and pointed over the road to the short street facing the hotel:

"Just a few yards along there, Sir. That's it: the old quaint-looking building," answered my father. He thanked us and proceeded in that direction. I observed that the building in question appeared more like an old chapel than a post office, and I said so to my father:

"It used to be a toll house at one time, son, because there was once a bridge spanning over a dene here. That is why they called it Barras Bridge."

"Is he going to post his dog, dad?" I asked, pondering on the reason for the luggage label attached to the animal's collar.

"He'll have a job getting that into the post-box, son. I think he's after

*Barras Bridge c1932*

taking some photos of the post office."

"What for Dad?" said I, more curious than ever.

"Because they're going to pull it down and build a bigger one, so I suppose he wants some photos as souvenirs."

The jumble sale remnants were not what my father had hoped for: three ladies' coats, some ladies' shoes and handbags, and a gent's umbrella. I was not surprised to learn that such good-looking handbags had remained unsold in the jumble sale. There would be very few women then living in Shieldfield who would have anything worthwhile to put in them, certainly not money. No doubt the bags would have been contributed by their better off sisters from up the road in Jesmond. My father put one pair of shoes and one of the coats aside. I guessed they were for my mother, and the rest would be sold to my Aunt Dolly:

"Why not keep one of those handbags for me mam?" I inquired. But my father peered at me in his particular fashion which I knew meant: When will you ever learn any sense? Of course I was aware that my mother, like a lot of other mams, had nothing of value to place in a handbag, but I was still convinced she would have liked one of these smart-looking bags even if it was only to keep photos in.

On leaving the church hall we crossed over into Jesmond, and began our business round the lanes of the private houses, my father calling out: "Any rags, woollens, or lumber for sale?"

What my father really meant was: "Have you got anything worthwhile to give away?" For all the tatters relied upon getting as many cast-offs as possible for nowt. Now my father, possessing a fine singing voice like myself, could not avoid calling out his business cries in such a rich musical tone that within minutes two or three women would come out into the lane, solely to look upon the owner of such a voice. Their token of appreciation however was always lost as far as my father was concerned. His empty pockets put him in no mood to be personally admired.

In one lane we were sitting on the shafts of the barrow having a breather. Up to that moment nothing had come our way in the line of business, and my father was appearing downcast. Suddenly a cat entered the lane from one of the backyards near to where we were resting, first peering up the lane and then down, as though to convince itself there were no other feline creatures in sight. It approached us in a confident manner. Without waiting for any signs of welcome from either of us, it sprang up onto the cart and began exploring the contents of it. My father, who was quite indifferent to cats, and only tolerated our own to please my mother and the children, alerted himself instantly and was about to brush it off the barrow with his hand, when a smart-looking woman aged about forty, appeared at the same door as the cat had come out of, and called out to the pussy. My father's intended swipe transformed itself swiftly into a gentle caress, and without turning around to even glance at the woman, he began whispering to the creature in an endearing pussy-cat lingo to which the cat responded favourably. This deliberate display of affection on the part of my father must have impressed the woman for she came over to us and addressed my father:

"I can see you love cats, mister," and she smiled on us pleasantly.

"I love them, my dear. They're my favourite animal. We have a one of our own at home, as my laddie can tell you."

Perhaps she will give us some rags and woollens now, I thought hopefully. The cat was now in the arms of its owner, being cradled like a baby, and the woman began quizzing my father, and attempting to size him up for some reason. Then suddenly she began discussing her aged father, whom she lived with. Indeed only the two of them were living in the fair-sized house:

"He's quite eccentric, poor soul. It's his age of course. I worry about his personal hygiene for he refuses point-blank to have a bath!"

At that age I was often hearing of someone in my own neighbourhood being described as 'eccentric', without coming to any conclusion about what the term meant. But on listening to this lady talking about her father, I wondered whether being 'eccentric', implied that the person so described was simply afraid of soap and water! Had he resided in our over-crowded billet, my father would soon have cured him of that complaint by the means of lifting him bodily into the poss-tub in our backyard once a week, and scrubbing him well with carbolic soap; the same kind of treatment that I and my brothers experienced whether we felt inclined for the pleasure or not.

After gaining my father's sympathy for her concern over her aged dad, she came out boldly with a ten-shilling proposition: to assist her dad in his 'predicament', as she described his distaste for bathing. My father's eyes lit up with joy at the size of the fee being offered. At the time he would have risked bathing a lion for ten-bob.

"He needs a good soaking, poor man," she emphasised. I knew my father was the one to see he got it.

It was a double-sized back door, which enabled us to take the barrow into the backyard, so avoiding my having to remain outside in the lane keeping sentinel on the barrow. The living room was nicely furnished and not overstocked like some of the posh houses I had been in. One could move around without any difficulty. What really struck me about the room was the absence of a fender or tidy: I couldn't remember ever entering a house that didn't possess those two fireside items. I would dearly have loved to offer the lady our own fender and tidy, for I was sick to death of having to work on it with emery paper until it gleamed like some treasure rescued from the pawnshop. A bird cage, on a stand situated near the window overlooking the backyard, housed a budgerigar. It began to display an excited curiousity at the sudden arrival of strangers, muttering its head off. I felt sure it was cursing our presence. Thankfully the lady put the kettle on and suggested we have some tea before the bathing session began: so much for the budgie's complaints, thought I. After she had spread the table with corned beef sandwiches and cherry cake, and filled our large breakfast cups with tea, she prepared a tray with a cup of tea and a piece of cake. Then she took it upstairs to her father, who we learned spent most of the day there, only descending in the evening to listen to the wireless for a couple of hours. When we had finished our meal, I was invited to accompany my father upstairs, the lady remarking that as her father liked children my presence would probably amuse him. Amuse him, thought I! She had some nerve. I was the one after seeking amusement. When we entered his large bedroom, which overlooked the street, the frail-looking old man was sitting at a small card-table playing at patience. He ignored us and continued his game. He was dressed in a gown over his pyjamas, and an odd-looking hat on his head, which I learned was called a fez. This head-dress gave him an oriental appearance. Apart from the crafty-faced old man, what interested me in the room was a large four poster bed complete with curtains.

"I've brought someone to assist you in the bathroom Father," said she.

He continued amusing himself with the cards not even deigning to glance sideways at us. I wondered whether he was hard of hearing; but surely this couldn't be so, for she would have raised her voice a little instead of speaking in her normal tone. Moving towards the bed she drew back the curtains and began searching for something: "Where have you placed the tray, Dad?" she inquired.

"What tray you talking about?" he retorted in a robust voice which belied his physical appearance.

"The one I brought up to you with tea and cake on it," she replied abruptly.

"You didn't bring me any tea or cake, that's another one of your fancies dear, just like your assertions that I need a bath. Me need a bath, humph, you can tell that one to the marines." Meanwhile his daughter continued looking for the concealed tray even peering under the bed for it. Finally she discovered it in the wardrobe. Placing the tray on the bed, she then whispered to my father, advising him to keep an eye on his jacket when he took it off to assist in the bathing. Her dad would conceal it in the most unlikely place if he got the opportunity.

"What are you whispering about my dear? Don't you dare plot against me, now then. I'm still master of this house and don't you forget it. I'm having no bath, and that's the end of it."

"Oh, shut up Dad," said she, appearing annoyed! Now before leading us upstairs, the lady had briefed my father, and given him to understand that under no circumstances was he to accept her father's expected refusal to take a bath as final. So long as he didn't hurt the old man in any way, he was to ignore his complaints.

Raising her voice slightly, for better effect, she addressed the old man: "I will go and run your bath Dad, and leave you to it."

She then turned to speak to my father: "My dad requires a little coaxing, but once he realises there is no alternative, you will find him no trouble at all."

"That's what you think," he called out as she was leaving the room. He rose from the table and going towards the bed a little unsteadily, sat on the edge facing us. After critically scrutinizing my father from head to feet, he cast his attention on to me, and inquired whether I had eaten all of the cherry cake downstairs.

"There's still half of it left in the cake tin," I replied and this information seemed to please him.

All the time he was addressing me, I was aware that my father was closely observing the old man, most probably attempting to ascertain whether he could encourage the pest to take to bath water voluntarily.

The daughter popped her head round the door: "The bath is all ready, Mister. Thank you." And we heard her descend the stairs afterwards.

"I believe your bath is ready Sir. Shall we get started?" asked my father, moving towards the bed. But the cunning old man had anticipated the move and fell backwards on the bed deliberately raising his legs into space and calling out:

"Leave me alone, you ruffian, or I will give you the biggest hiding you've ever had in your life."

My father beckoned to me and pointed towards the old man's slippers, whispering: "Take his slippers off, son, and watch your head in case he kicks out."

I swiftly removed the slippers before he could recollect his wits, but no sooner had I done that than he slipped off to the other side of the bed and crawled underneath it.

"It's going to be a hard ten bob's worth, son," remarked my father wearily. I got down on my knees, and first removing the chamber pot from the grasp of the old man, I addressed him in a soothing tone:

"Come on an' have a bath, Mister, soap and water won't harm you." He raised a fist and shook it in anger:

"I'll harm you, you little imp, if I get my hands on you," he retorted. "Give me back my slippers you little thief."

"You'll have to come out for them," I replied. My father who was by the other side of the bed decided also to get down on his knees to plead:

"If you don't come out from under the bed, Sir, I'll have to move it to get at you. I'm only following your daughter's instructions. Goodness me, a bath won't harm you."

"Then why don't you go and get into it," replied he in a sarcastic manner. "I don't require a bath. And you shouldn't take your commission too seriously Mister, nor the word of my daughter if it comes to that."

My father appeared frustrated, but truthfully I was enjoying the antics of the old man for I had never before witnessed any adult perform in the way he was doing, except on the cinema screen. Of course I ensured that my father did not sense I was enjoying myself. Suddenly my father made his mind up to put an end to the game of hide-and-seek. Taking my cue from him, I stood up and pulled the bed towards me as he pushed it in the same direction. Then he stooped swiftly, and firmly but gently picked up the old man as though lifting a child and placed him on the bed:

"I'm sorry Sir, but I can't afford to waste my time. I've got a family to look after; and you're going to have a bath."

The old man appeared completely dismayed. He shrugged his shoulders and made no attempt to resist for he seemed to realise my father was in no mood for fooling around or tolerating his tantrums. However it soon transpired he had not given up hope of avoiding being well and truly soaked.

"How is the scrap business doing these days?" he inquired; which proved he must have been observing us from one of the back bedroom windows as we entered the backyard with our barrow.

"Very poor, Sir. There are too many of us at the game these days," replied my father, making a move to divest him of his dressing gown. The old man placed his hands over my father's as though urging him to bide his time a few seconds:

"Listen to me my man," he whispered, "I don't need a bath, and I'm quite sure you don't particularly wish to give me one; so why bother to satisfy the whims of a foolish woman..." Placing a finger to his lips as a pledge of secrecy, he freed himself from my father's grasp, and moved up to the head of the bed where he lifted up the bolster to reveal a purse. He took out of it two half-crowns and handed them to my father: "Here, place those into your pocket, and let us go into the bathroom and create the impression for my daughter, downstairs, that I'm having a bath; then downstairs you go yourself, and be paid whatever she promised you." On observing my father hesitating, he added: "If you do attempt to give me a bath, Mister, you'll have to employ force, and let me warn you, I possess good lungs, and I'll shout so loud that all the neighbours in the street will be out to investigate."

My father pocketed the bribe in the face of such determination; probably pleased to settle the issue more favourably than he expected. As he informed me later, he had known some people who had abstained from bathing for years without displaying any signs of discomfort; not that such a way of life would ever appeal to him personally.

The old man removed his dressing gown and placed it on the bed with his hat, and led the way to the bathroom. When I saw the lay-out of the bathroom I became envious of the luxurious comfort that was wasted on someone who appeared to be repelled even at the sight of the place. There was a nice snug-looking rug on the floor, towels galore, sponges, a large bath brush, bath salts, and various brands of soap. This was my first experience of being in a real bathroom and I wouldn't have had to be tempted much to plunge into the water myself if given the opportunity.

The sly old coot placed one of the towels onto the door handle so as it covered the keyhole, in case his daughter crept upstairs and attempted to peep; a wise precaution of course for none of us, especially my father, wished to be caught in the deception. While the old man sat on the stool humming to himself, my father talked out loud sounding as though he was praising the old man for giving himself a good soak. Meanwhile I was continually washing my hands and swishing the bath water about, and drying them on two of the towels to give the impression that they had been used for bathing. With regard to the old man himself, the only water he would consent to have contact with was to dip the hairbrush into the bath and dress his hair to create the impression that he had washed it. After a reasonable time, I took the plug out and washed the bath until it shone like a mirror. That was more than I could have done with our wooden poss-tub back home where my brothers and I were bathed.

Before my father and I went downstairs, the old man got us to promise that if we were offered any more cherry cake we would refuse if, as it was his favourite. But when we did arrive back in the parlour, the good lady made us coffee and even encouraged me to dispose of the remainder of the cherry cake (probably in order to spite her father) and I required very little tempting. Afterwards she handed over the promised ten-shilling note, and gave me threepence, and before leaving the house she invited my father to call again the next time he was in the area.

Back in the lane we recommenced tatting. In the distance we heard the sound of a bugle! Although the usual call of most rag merchants was vocal only: "Any rags, woollens, or scrap for sale?" there were those hawkers who earned themselves the tag of 'pest', not only from the public at large, but from other rag men: these were the bugle men. Their arrival in any lane disturbed those individuals fortunate enough to be in employment, but unfortunate to be on nightshift and so hoping to be able to sleep during the day. The instant one of these men blasted off with their wretched bugle, every canine creature in that lane, whether they were indoors or out, would begin howling in distress and sounding as though they were attempting to rouse the ghosts of their primitive ancestors. Then the womenfolk would come out into the lane and all hell would break loose.

Owing to the fact that there were too many hawkers and the competition was too brisk, every tatter was always hoping, even praying, that any lumber to come their way would be given to them free; and with the poor prices being paid by the wholesale merchants, it was only natural. The most these men could afford to part with in return for rags or lumber was a balloon secured to a stick. My father always ensured that he had a stock of loose balloons in his pockets, but his main give-away to the kids in the working-class districts were comics received from people in the affluent areas of the city. One thing he would not deal with was goldfish, for apart from the inconvenience of carting them around, he was against such barter on principle, looking upon it as a form of unnecessary cruelty.

Two hours after leaving the house in a contented mood, our cart was loaded with a good quality fender and tongs, a large bathroom mirror, a stock of woollens and the large sack was full of cast-off clothing too good to be described as rags, all gained at the cost of a few balloons to the kids. My father began smoking his last Woodbine in the remarkable style of a playboy of the western world. I could almost see the reflection of half-pint glasses of Bass in the pupils of his smiling eyes, for surely the thought of the coming evening's liquid pleasures had set him off singing softly to himself *The Rose of Tralee*. This was his favourite song which he often sang on a Saturday evening in front of the mirror when he was dressing to go to town on those rare occasions only possible when the day's fiddling had been profitable.

*Jesmond Road in the 1920s*

Soon it was time for us to proceed to City Road in quest of the bread hand-out. At the horse trough on Jesmond Road, another tatter, a full-time professional who owned a furniture shop in Byker, was allowing his horse to have a drink, and my father stopped to have a few words with him. As they talked shop, the hawker kept admiring the bathroom mirror, then remarked on it:

"Nice mirror you got there, Jimmy. If you're not thinking of keeping it, I'll give you four shillings for it." I was delighted that my father agreed to sell, for my arms were weary through having to ensure it did not come to any mishap. I approached the poor old workhorse and stroked its mane, gently uttering a few kind words of comfort. God knows all such creatures need it. All graft, very little grub, and no romping about in a meadow after the day's end, only back to some mean grubby stable and forgotten until the following morning.

After the hawker had transferred the mirror to his own cart and left us, I watched curiously as my father dipped his hands into the trough and deliberately dried them on the woollens. When I asked him why he did it, he remarked: "It's an old trick of the trade son; it increases the weight of the woollens."

When we arrived on City Road I remained with the barrow, out of sight, while my father entered the bakery where the exhibition had been held. When he returned he was carrying a large sugar bag on his back, full of bread.

Outside the wholesale merchants in Gallowgate, the usual sad-faced loungers were patiently waiting each tatter in turn. By being allowed to look over the contents of the carts, they hoped to come across an item of clothing or footwear which they knew would cost them that little bit less than having to purchase from the secondhand shops. It mattered little if the tatter concerned was of the opinion that the clothing on his cart was fit for only the rag-bag: he would learn that there were those who were prepared, through necessity, to sit and darn their nights away in order to restore some semblence of respectability to the most tattered garment on his cart!

My father was ready as the men and women approached his barrow. What serviceable clothing there was to fit the needs of our own family had already been secured. It was the two ladies' coats from the jumble sale remnants that first attracted every one of the seekers. A man and woman both took hold of one of them and began wrangling over it but my father diplomatically relieved them of it:

"Let the lady try it on first, Mister," said he. "If it doesn't fit her, then you can have your say as to whether it would fit your missus or not."

The woman eagerly tried on the coat, and claimed it did fit. I reckoned that a few more helpings of leek-pudding and mince-and-dumplings inside her would improve the look of it. By then the last remaining coat had been sold. I soon realised that my Aunt would not be setting her eyes upon any of the ladies' shoes either, for they were being haggled over as well. Only three pairs of shoes remained unsold: the high-heeled type. The others had been sensible footwear, the kind which these women would require for their every-day trudging around the shops, looking for knock-down bargains. The nice-looking handbags attracted envious sighs, but no offers. One or two of the women had given them a wistful examination, fondly stroking them as though they were delightful kittens, but they had to be rejected, for their lives were strictly controlled by priorities, and handbags were not one of them. After all, they were only ornaments if one had nothing to put in them.

The man, who had been unfortunate in the woman's coat dispute, snapped up a pair of stays and asked the price of them. Before my father could reply, another woman, who had been on the point of picking them up demanded: "Why divint you ask your missis to come herself an' choose her things?"

The man peered at her so furiously that it seemed as though he would strike her, but instead he replied piteously:

"Because she's not well, that's why," then in a change of tone: "if it has anything to do with you, busybody."

Paying for the stays, he concealed them under his jacket and hurried away from his apparent tormentors.

When my father had gone into the rag depot with the worst of his lumber, the woman who had wanted the stays, inquired of me: "What's in that other bag, son, could I have a look in?"

I realised that if I was silly enough to admit that the sack was full of wholemeal bread, there could be a riot in Gallowgate: "I don't know what's in it, missis. You better ask my Dad when he comes back."

She made to prod the sack to have her curiosity satisfied, but I intercepted her, and whispered: "I didn't want to tell you, missus, but there's a deed dog in the sack, our dog. It got run over on Jesmond Road an' we're takin' it to the Cat and Dog Shelter."

She almost jumped away from the barrow with apparent shock:

"A deed dog! I think your father ought to have gone to the Shelter, first. Coming here with deed dogs." And off she went, the rest of the gathering following her, just as my father was approaching.

"I'll get going to your Aunt Dolly's son, with this fender and the rest of the things. Here's a penny for the tram. As soon as you finish delivering your papers come straight home. I'll have a good tea ready for you."

*Trams on Benwell Lane*

On the tram, I ruminated as to whether remaining away from school and missing out on my free lunch had been worth it. I couldn't quite make my mind up; not that I'd had much option. It had been an interesting day I supposed. But I decided that when I grew up, I would never become a tatter. My choice would rest upon my three long-held ambitions: to be a singer, a blacksmith or a cowboy.

# Christmas 1934

Christmas Eve! Tomorrow would be my tenth Christmas on earth. The first Christmas I had any recollection of was when I was four. Circumstances hadn't improved any since that time, in fact, due to family increase, there were now ten of us including my parents, and things were worse. To augment the situation over the previous two weeks my father had failed almost completely to make any money on his tatting round.

It didn't seem like a Monday morning, as I made my way along the terrace towards the newsagent's shop. It seemed more like a Saturday, for the proprietors of the fruit shops, and Storey's, the hardware shop, were busy erecting their trestle tables on the forecourts outside their premises in preparation for the Christmas shoppers. By eight o'clock I was almost finished my paper round so I sat on the garden wall to take a breather and have my usual morning glance through the *Journal*. The headlines of one of its main articles attracted my attention:

"IT WILL BE A MERRIER CHRISTMAS TIDE. MORE MONEY IN CIRCULATION!"

I read on, hopefully. But all I learned was that the city shop tills were ringing merrily and working overtime. I didn't get to know precisely who was doing all the spending, though I was confident that with few exceptions no one in my neighbourhood was engaged in the reported spending spree. Further down the paper I observed that the King was to give his Christmas broadcast next day from Sandringham at 3 p.m.! But then we didn't possess a wireless, so I wouldn't hear what he might have to say about there being more money in circulation.

However, I could look forward to one treat on Christmas day. A free breakfast was to be held in the Bond Street Memorial Church Hall. My elder sister, and one of my brothers were also going. I hadn't worked out whether the three of us had been invited on account of our periodic visits to the Sunday School, or because we were members of a large family, for I was aware that the Bond Street Memorial Church did dispense charity to needy people. Then again, I was on speaking terms with the Vicar: he was one of my regular firewood customers. Whenever I called to deliver his supply, his good wife always provided me with a chunk of mouth-watering cake. The vicar sometimes presented me with a religious picture card which I added to my collection, and allowed my young sister to keep for me!

When I got back home, my mother and elder sister were waiting for me, and so we set off to the terrace to join in this reported spending spree. Our first call was at the butcher's shop for a rabbit for the Christmas dinner! It didn't look big enough for ten of us to feast on; a ten-legged rabbit would have been ideal. Having changed the pound note, my mother give me the necessary coppers, and I left them to begin my hunt for some spare-rib bones for the dinner on Boxing Day, and some cracked eggs. I scored for the eggs at Duncan's stores, then it took me three more trips on the terrace, first the Co-op, then Law's Stores, and finally Hadrian's, before I could get the spare ribs for the broth, and bacon pieces for other meals. As we trudged up the street laden with our carrier-bags, I remarked: "We've got plenty of stuff, haven't we mam?"

She sighed wearily: "We'll be lucky if we have anything left for tea on Boxing Day."

After my father had fried some of the bacon pieces, and my mother was busy making up the sandwiches, I went out into the lane to call my brothers in for lunch. Only my young sister had the rind cut off the bacon, the rest of us wouldn't think of such waste. We left it to our digestive systems to decide whether it could be assimilated or not. Being a bread-winner, I always got a mug of tea to myself, but my brothers, due solely to the lack of drinking utensils, had to share one cup between two of them. I would have sooner been considered for an extra sandwich and share my tea, but when it came to grub distribution, my father was very exact: no favouritism.

After lunch I prepared to go out on my firewood round, despite my parents suggesting I forego it and go out and play with my pals. I reminded them that I would have all the next day to myself as there were no newspapers printed on Christmas Day. Furthermore, I realised that my customers would be in their usual seasonal mood, and my stomach had ample space after my frugal lunch to accommodate any mince pies or other Christmas delicacies that might be offered to me.

Before we went to bed that night, each one of us handed our mother one of our stockings. She in turn passed them over to our father, who secured them to the clothes line over the range by the means of safety-pins. With the exception of my elder sister and myself, the children took turns to make known to Santa Claus what they wanted for Christmas by calling up the chimney. My elder sister, who was two years older than myself, had confided in me earlier in the day that she had given up Santa Claus for lost, reminding me that neither of us could ever remember when he paid us a visit! When I climbed into the double bed that I was sharing with my three brothers in the other room, my brother John was all ready to quiz me: "Why didn't you shout up the chimney to tell Santa Claus what you wanted for Christmas?"

I realised I had better not admit that I now doubted whether Santa Claus was alive, for that would start a right rumpus, and bring my father into the bedroom and probably earn me a wallop; so I claimed I had called up the chimney earlier in the day.

"What did you ask for?" demanded Walter.

"I asked for a cowboy outfit, and a pair of shoes," said I.

"What do you want a cowboy outfit for?" asked John.

"Because I'm sick of pretending I'm dressed like a cowboy, when the other kids have got real gun belts and guns and hats," I retorted. "So shut up, and let me get to sleep."

Then I asked my brother Arthur, to remove his foot from my chin, which was an almost impossible request; four pairs of feet in one bed can create problems.

Normally on holidays and Sunday mornings, none of my brothers were allowed out of bed before eight-thirty. I was the exception to the rule, for apart from having to do my paper-round, I was the chosen fire-builder, a supposed honour invested upon me by my father, on account of my being a cowboy. Getting a fire going had to be the first task of the day whatever the season, for without a fire to heat the water in the set-pot, to heat the oven for baking, and to boil kettles and pans, life in our two-room billet would be impossible. However, on a Christmas morning my father always relaxed the time-to-rise restriction, and everyone was allowed to rise by seven o'clock. But one rule he never relaxed: the soap and water roll-call! Time I built the fire, my father, an early riser at all times, and having completed his own cold-water wash at the sink, began supervising my brothers having theirs. One at a time they went out on to the stairhead, and returned visibly shivering and eager to grab hold of the communal towel and briskly rub themselves in their haste to restore their circulation. My two sisters were excused this spartan exercise; they simply rubbed their hands with a flannel, and waited until the water in the set-pot was hot enough so as they could complete their ablutions. Afterwards each one of us was handed our stocking, containing an apple, orange and some nuts. On realising the doll she had ordered from Santa Claus hadn't materialised, my young sister Mary began crying. This set off my two younger brothers. My mother began attempting to pacify my sister; my father warned my brothers, either cease crying or go back to bed. After peace had been restored, my father explained that the chimney was too narrow for Santa Claus to come down, especially with a bag of toys; and he promised he would look for a bigger house with a larger chimney, in time for next Christmas. If I'd had the courage, I could have asked my father what prevented Santa Claus from coming up the stairs and leaving our presents on the stairhead, but I wasn't prepared to risk a box on the ears for my display of wisdom.

At nine o'clock sharp, Kitty, Arthur and myself, were sprinting along the terrace towards the Bond Street Memorial Church hall. It was a delight to enter the brightly-lit, centrally-heated, decorated hall. As we entered, we were each given a paper hat and a Christmas cracker, then directed to one of the long trestle-tables. By nine-thirty, the hall was full, and the volunteer staff, led by the Vicar and his wife, came around distributing a meat-square and a bag of cakes to each one of us! We couldn't begin to lower this mouth-watering food into our permanently hungry stomachs, until the good Vicar climbed onto the stage and led us in saying Grace. This had most of us in such a shuffle that the good man was glad to jump on to the stage as though the devil himself was chasing him. In three seconds flat we thanked God for what we were about to receive then attacked the grub as though we bore a delightful grudge against it, in as much that the sooner it was out of sight and lodged in our stomachs the better we would all like it. Back came the cheery ladies, with huge teapots this time. Thank heaven my liver was in good fettle, for I knew by past experience that all charity tea was of a potent vintage; times were hard, but there was always great liberality in the mashing of this popular brew. My father would have been in his glory having numerous pots of this special charity tea being served out to him; for tea at home, like everything else, was always in short supply.

The Vicar, bless him, also adorned in a paper hat, was strolling about the hall encouraging us to enjoy ourselves, and even attempting to entice us in the impossible feat of singing Carols as we were munching cakes and consuming strong tea. For most of us present this morning party was our only experience of Christmas, and if given the choice I think we would have opted to remain in the hall until bedtime. But this once-a-year bountiful occasion came to a close far too soon: after all, the Vicar and his band of jolly volunteers would have other things to do. And we filed out into the cold to go back to our overcrowded billets.

Back home I crawled under the double bed in the living room to be out of the way, pretending I was in a cave in Arizona, miles from anywhere and from any living soul. But my day-dreaming was cut short; living space being at a premium, I was joined by John and Walter:

"Tell us a story, like the ones you tell us in bed," asked John.

Just as I was about to begin a ghost story, I was hailed from my lair by my father:

"Here, take this jug, and the sixpence, and go across to Crawford's and get some Bass, and no drinking of it, do your hear me?"

"Yes Dad. I won't touch it. I don't like it." You can believe that if you wish, thought I.

There was not a soul in sight in the street, not even a stray mongrel or a pussy cat. I had always thought there was something uncanny about Christmas Day. Where did all the people go? Even Mrs Rubbing-Stone was absent from sight. The tinkle of the shop door bell brought Mr Crawford in from the back kitchen:

"A jug of Bass, Mr Crawford, please. An' Merry Christmas."

"I've told you before, Tommy, you ought to give up drinking," said he, as he took the jug from me.

I wondered whether he ever sampled his beers, he always appeared too sober to me. I knew one Off-Licence proprietor, down in Elswick, who by now (eleven-thirty) would be drunk as a noodle in his cellar, time his overworked wife would be filling the neighbourhood's jugs. The young son, a pal of mine, on the pretence of keeping a protective eye on his dad, would be draining what profits his father had left, by consuming as much ginger beer and other soft drinks as his system could hold.

As Mr Crawford was filling my jug, Mr Wilson entered the shop with his oversized jug. He was dressed in trousers, slippers and an open shirt, yet the temperature outside was low enough to inconvenience the hardiest of Eskimos. He glanced at me as though seeing me for the first time in his life:

"Do you live about here, son?" he asked.

"Well I only live two doors away from you," I remarked looking puzzled. "I sometimes gan for your baccy to Broyd's, at the top of the street."

Mr Crawford handed me the jug of beer and I passed him the money. To my surprise he gave me a Christmas cracker which he had on the shelf behind him next to a miniature Christmas tree.

"You say you go to Broyd's for me baccy? Alright then, what do they call me?" asked Mr Wilson, as he handed his own jug over the counter to be filled.

"They call you Mr Wilson, an' you live two doors from us," I replied. I detected Mr Crawford winking at me; then it dawned on me that Mr Wilson was drunk, and most probably didn't know what day it was. I was surprised that his missis had allowed him out without a coat on in such weather, for since his accident in the pit, he had never been the same man.

"Thank God, I've got nee kids," he muttered as I went out of the shop.

After dinner was over, and my father had drained the jug dry, he was in a much better mood, and brought out his mouth-organ from the press. Some of us sat on the fender and the rest of us on the mat, enthralled at the idea that we were going to be entertained to a musical treat, for our father was a grand player. We all agreed he should play Christmas Carols, and those of us who knew the words formed the family choir, led by our mother. She had been in the Salavation Army at Blaydon when she was a young lass, and possessed a fine voice; she still loved to sing the 'Army songs', especially on a Sunday when she was baking.

Before we went to bed that night, our father picked up his library book and read to us all about Scrooge the miser, by Charles Dickens. I was almost annoyed to hear of the meanness of this old skinflint; but I was quick to respond, along with my brothers and sisters, to the delightful change of heart that Marley's ghost brought about in him.

# The Chimney Sweep

Ill as we could afford it, we were expecting a call from the local chimney sweep, and when anyone in our almost permanent state of insolvency had to resort to call upon his services, one can rest assured it was as the last resort. My father had tried every device short of setting the house on fire, which, incidently, would have resulted in making at least three families homeless. And a fire in the grate we must have, for it was the only source of generating domestic heat! The fender, tongs, poker and the kettle were safely out of harm's way under the double bed in the living room, and my sisters and brothers were in the other room occupying themselves as well as they could in the limited space there, for a double bed and a single one took up most of it. The cat had been sent packing downstairs into the lane to try its luck with the fishmonger who at that moment was calling out how cheap and excellent his kippers and fishcakes were. As for myself, I was present at the immediate scene of impending activity in case the sweep required a little assistance. If he did, it would have to be on a very limited scale indeed. There would be no question of me climbing up the chimney supposing we never more had a fire in the grate! I was aware that little Oliver Twist avoided such a fate by falling to his knees in front of the magistrate and begging for mercy, much to the annoyance of the penny-pinching villainous workhouse committee, who desired to have him signed-over to the penny-pinching villainous sweep. Well there would be no danger of me falling to my knees and pleading for mercy, for I had decided beforehand that if I had to poke my head up the chimney I would scarper and take to the road like a gipsy.

There was such a loud rap on the outside of the living room door that I felt sure it was the Police, arriving to apprehend my father and ship him off to Botany Bay for having set fire to the chimney the previous evening in an unsuccessful attempt to avoid having to engage the sweep. My father strode towards the door so swiftly and appeared so annoyed at such a loud summons, that I was expecting him to either throttle or throw down the stairs whoever was calling. It was the sweep, and my father managed to

*Mr R. W. Frame, Chimney Sweep, at work in Newcastle, 1934*

suppress his irritation. The bulky, soot-covered individual entered without a word, his form of greeting being a wide friendly smile. One thing was certain in my mind, this man would require a huge wide chimney to accommodate his dimensions; he would probably fit into the chimney of some mansion, but the chimney spaces in our district were as limited as living space and family income.

"Having trouble with the chimney, aye?" he asked, after laying down his kit on the floor, which resulted in a film of black dust rising from it and settling on the floor to as far as the bed. "Having trouble with the chimney?" he repeated, as though seeking a definite response.

My mother answered him in the affirmative. Had he depended on my father to reply to such an obvious query or comment, whichever it was meant to be, he would have overstayed his logging time. On realising that he did not climb up into the chimney, I was amazed at the state he was in for he was as black as the ace of spades; no mine-worker on face-work could have collected so much carbonaceous dust on his person:

"Well it won't take me long to get this job finished, hinny," said he addressing my mother, yet continuing to move at a speed as though he intended taking all day to accomplish the task.

Opening his large sack, he brought out his bundle of rods, brush-head, dust-cover and a small shovel. Placing the cover around the fireplace he secured it by means of the flat-iron and a couple of firebricks to the mantle-shelf. In the centre of this large cover was a kind of mouth or sleeve through which he began inserting in turn his rods, fitting them together by means of the brass rings on the end of each rod. He was about to fit the third rod on when it dawned upon him that he would have to dismantle the others because he had forgotten to fit the brush on to the first rod:

"We all make mistakes, don't we?" he remarked to no one in particular.

"That can't be helped hinny," said my mother hoping to appease him. But the truth was that he obviously required no comforting, for he appeared to be the most complacent man I had ever seen. I don't think any mortal thing could have seriously bothered him, and regarding the question of time, I believe he was indifferent to it. One could easily have been led to assume that he must have possessed private means, and that his following the occupation of sweep was solely to gratify some unusual whim of his. Finally he accomplished fitting together as many rods as were necessary for an upstairs flat:

"Well, it won't take me long now to get the job finished, Mister," said he, turning round from the fireplace to address my father directly, as though pondering whether it was possible to obtain some rapport with him.

"I'm glad to hear that," replied my father. "Saturday must be a busy day for you. It certainly is for me and my missis, to get the shopping in."

I glanced up at my father thinking to myself: that will be the day, when you go a message! He was a good grafter mind you, not in the least afraid of work, but shopping he wouldn't do, that was left for my mother and myself.

"No, I'm never too busy on a Saturday, Mister. I usually knock-off about twelve o'clock," said the sweep, halting his actions once more to turn round to face my father.

"You finish at twelve o'clock, do you?" remarked my father in a dry manner, as though implying: if you don't get a move on, it will be midnight before you finish!

"I mean twelve-noon, you know," said the sweep, suddenly laughing loud in a most jovial manner and appearing to refute any thoughts my father may be holding to the contrary.

Soot and more solid matter were by now landing in the fireplace as the sweep began withdrawing the rods and unscrewing them. Gently he released one of the corners of the soot cloth and peered behind it:

"That's it. It won't take me long now." With his small shovel he began filling the sack with the debris. At that moment one of my brothers peeped-in from the other room and my father advised him:

"Stop in there John, just now, and tell the others too."

The sweep hesitated in what he was doing to inquire of my father how many children he had.

"Eight!" replied he, sounding weary; though whether this was because of the man's slow rate of progress, or at having to remind himself of the actual size of his family, I couldn't tell.

After the sweep had taken the bag of soot downstairs into the yard he returned to collect his rods, which he placed inside his cover cloth, and secured together with a leather strap. Then came the moment of reckoning, so we thought. My father handed him the fee, but the sweep looking more than ever now like a Kentucky-Minstrel, as he displayed his white teeth, for he was smiling good-naturedly, shook his head in a gentle and dismissive manner:

"Put it back in your pocket, Mister, you have more than enough to do with your means. I assure you I'm not lacking in a bob or two. Furthermore, if you ever have any trouble with your chimney, don't hesitate to come to me and I'll see you alright, that's a promise. Good day to you all."

"Will you have a cup of tea?" asked my father, who like my mother, and myself, was taken aback by the rather unexpected and kind gesture of the man.

"No, no, but thanks. I'll let you get on with putting the place to rights." And off he went, down the stairs, humming some tune in a contented manner.

# Sunday Morning on the Quayside

We had now moved from Benwell, and were well settled in the district of Elswick, near to Scotswood Road. Life was easier for all of us; we now had three rooms in a downstairs flat, complete with scullery and gas-cooker, and the added bonus of a backyard to ourselves!

It was one of the neighbours in our lane who first told me about the Sunday morning Quayside market, and the colourful characters that congregated there, so I discreetly questioned him on how one got there?

"Well, nipper. Gan doon the lane an' catch a tramcar, an' get off at the Central Station, then go ..." I interrupted him, for like most adults I knew of, he was assuming that it was only possible to get anywhere by boarding a tramcar:

"I never have money for tramfares, Mister. How can you get there by walking? Is it straight along Scotswood Road?" He began scratching his head in a bewildered manner:

"Walkin' hinny! Neebody walks that far if they've got any sense. Yeh better forget aboot the Quayside until yeh leave school an' start work an' get some pocket money."

He hadn't been much assistance, but I did manage to get him to admit that the quayside wasn't far from the Central Station.

One Sunday morning soon after, I remarked I was off to Elswick Park to play at cowboys. I was willing to chance having my bait put up (an expression used by my father whenever he was promising me a good hiding for any possible misdemeanour of mine). Once on Scotswood Road, I pretended I was on my favourite horse and set off at a gallop. Arriving at the Cattle Market I made an inquiry from one of the street-corner men, who directed me to go down Forth Bank then turn left.

I arrived on the Quayside beside the Swing Bridge! I stood fascinated: the scene reminded me of the Town Moor Hoppings in Race Week. The long snake-like chain of stalls, with the odd van and lorry protruding here and there was a sight beyond all my expectations. Although I was financially insolvent and therefore unable to supply my neglected stomach with any of the many brands of ice cream, fruit or soft drinks available, this would not prevent me from feasting my curiousity and whatever intellect I possessed on all those quaint characters I had heard tell of. I began my adventure by glancing at some of the individuals aiming darts at pinned-up playing cards and hoping to win a small prize. Next to that stall stood a group who were lubricating their throats with fruity-looking drinks at a penny a glass. My close attention was called for when I arrived at one particular lorry which

*The Quayside Market c1935*

was being utilised as a fruit stall, run by three brothers. Number-one-brother was standing on the quay in the forefront of the large crowd gathered in front of the stall. His job, I observed, was to hand out the goods and collect the cash from the customers. Of the two men on board the lorry, brother-number-two was being kept busy opening up boxes of various fruits. The third brother was the patter-merchant and he never ceased talking as he filled the carrier bags with fruit. His delivery was so swift that he could not avoid spittle spraying number-one-brother, standing directly below him, whose objections were totally ignored.

"Now then, lads an' lasses, I want you all to taak note what's goin' into the carrier bags, 'cause I'm no Palace Theatre magician tryin' to pull the wool over your eyes. An' you'll get no bruised fruit here, top quality is what I buy or nowt at all. First: a dozen oranges. Next: a dozen Mackingtosh reds, lovely apples I tell you, followed by six juicy calabash pears, a hand of bananas, an' grapes..."

"How aboot a lemon?" called out a man from the crowd.

"You look sour enough hinny, withoot suckin' a lemon," retorted brother-three.

"Now then, never mind a half-crown, or two-bob, not even one-an'-a'-tanner. Here! First come first served, a bob the lot. An' for goodness sake divint all rush at once an' crush wor kid doon there, for he's very delicate."

Despite the immediate profitable response to his sales offer, he appeared eager and determined to increase the demand for the shilling lot, for he suddenly ceased filling the carrier bags for a brief moment and began throwing samples of oranges and apples out to the crowd, hoping to influence the doubters.

"Here, taste those an' see the value of what you're buyin'."

He certainly influenced me with his fruit shower. The temptation was too great and so I ignored all the rules of the game and fair play. Within seconds I had caught two apples and an orange before any of the brothers had collected their wits. Then suddenly brother-number-one attempted to grab me, but I was already pushing my way out of the crowd:

"If I catch hold of you, you little waster..." his voice faded as I swiftly ran from sight.

Munching one of the apples, I made my way along the quay, and came upon a long stall stacked high with household merchandise with its proprietor, an Ali-Baba-looking character, perched upon his platform declaiming the reason why he had to work seven days a week. I formed the opinion that he was worth a few minutes of my time. According to him, he had five wives in India, and one in Newcastle, besides having numerous children in both places. My first impression was that he had travelled a terrible long way from India to earn a living selling the kind of merchandise that could be purchased from any drapery stall in the Grainger Market. He had begun to fold a pair of double-sized sheets which he had been displaying, when his shrewd dark eyes peered down on me. He ceased his activities to address me:

"You! Yes you. You little monkey, why you not at church? Never mind:

get hold of this end of sheet and stop idling the time away."

I eagerly stepped forward to assist him in folding the sheets, hoping he might engage my services for the morning, but as soon as the task was complete, he appeared to forget I was still there. Nonetheless, I stood my ground a little while, for I realised he was a man who could make a seemingly dull occupation appear and sound like some variety act, simply by good humouredly insulting his audience and would-be customers, who were obviously lapping it up and enjoying every moment of it.

Directly under the new Tyne Bridge, which had been in use for just over six years, I observed a one-legged jeweller, exhibiting his goods on a card table, and I learned that this was Harry the Jew, who had a jeweller's shop up in town. This fact alone, I supposed, established his market reputation, for he certainly appeared content to display his goods without indulging in any form of open-air salesmanship. What particularly interested me about this one-legged businessman, was his ability, just like that of 'Long John Silver', to move about quite freely and efficiently with the aid of only one crutch. I was surprised that in his kind of trade he found it profitable to attend the Quayside market at times of deep depression. But I was even more surprised when two men, all in the space of five minutes of each other, purchased a gold ring each. It puzzled me that anyone could spend so much money on small bands of metal, and I formed the opinion that they wanted their heads examining. However, apart from these two individuals, who undoubtedly had arrived on the scene with the intention to purchase gold rings, the majority of the morning strollers passed his stall, giving but a glance to his glittering array of jewellery. Perhaps like myself, they were searching out the colourful characters to be amused by. And my next stop, was to observe just such a one. He too could be described as a jeweller of sorts, though his stock in trade that morning consisted solely of Swiss pocket watches, which he was offering for sale at one shilling and elevenpence each. To listen to this man, one would assume that the watches he was after selling had been made specifically for his business alone. He appeared to be acquainted with a fair history of clock and watch making, at least as far as the Swiss were concerned. It impressed me that any man could root a crowd round his stall where the only object on view was a cheaply-priced pocket watch. So confident was this man of his merchandise, that he was offering every intending customer a guarantee that he would reimburse anyone the full price if the watch was to develop any fault within three months of purchase. And like all good salesmen he possessed a good line of patter, a little far-fetched at times, but amusing:

"Ladies and gentlemen, let me tell you: the Duke of Wellington won the battle of Waterloo mainly through synchronised timing as well as other factors. Napoleon, on the other hand, lost due to faulty timing. Wellington possessed and always relied upon his Swiss-made watch; furthermore, his watch and those of his Officers, were made by the very same firm that today manufactures the watches I'm selling on this Quayside. Napoleon swore, and lost, by relying upon his French-made watch. My friends, the French can make excellent Cognac, but I assure you, they cannot make reliable timepieces. And I also assure you, no railwayman would be without his Swiss-made pocket watch."

He claimed that all prominent individuals such as boxing-ring timekeepers, football referees, racing-car drivers, policemen, judges, and hangmen, relied upon their Swiss-made watches for accuracy. And of course, all of them were manufactured by the same firm that he dealt with.

Until this particular morning, I had never realised that buskers worked on a Sunday, but half way along the chain of stalls I recognised a character playing his accordian. He was a regular visitor to my own district, mainly on a Saturday afternoon. After listening to a few tunes, I moved forward and introduced myself to him, telling him where I lived and how I looked forward to his appearance in my backlane. He was very polite to me but didn't seem too impressed. It never dawned on me that my holding a conversation with him was delaying his business, but it didn't take him long to remind me of the fact. Taking the hint, I moved back to the kerbside and sat down to eat my remaining apple, and the orange.

Next to the stall of Harry the Boot King was a huge African gentleman who by his commanding appearance, diction, and rich bass voice, reminded me of Paul Robeson. He was the first quack doctor I had ever set eyes upon, though I was to learn, a little later, that there were others present. I discreetly pushed my way into the front of his audience. Soon I became enthralled at his performance, for no Hollywood actor ever played the part of a mountebank as convincingly and as smoothly as this fine looking man: he was unique and of an Oscar-winning calibre. Whatever medical knowledge he did really possess that was worthwhile, one thing appeared certain, he was well versed in the basics of herbs and their medicinal qualities, though the powers he was ascribing to particular herbs were more magical than curative. According to him, there were herbs for every complaint that man is prone to, providing they are taken in time: "Learn from the animals!" appeared to be one of his popular phrases:

"When you are feeling poorly and are off your food, I say to you: do as your forefathers did before you, visit the countryside and collect the herbs. And for goodness sake keep away from the doctor's surgery; keep off the trash that is served up by the chemist shops; remember, the countryside is nature's laboratory!"

A narrow-shouldered and shallow-chested man standing next to me suddenly broke out in a fit of coughing, no doubt due to the fag-end he had just lit up. The herbal-doctor ceased in mid-sentence and instantly cast his expert attention on to the victim. It became obvious that he was determined to make use of such a bronchial outburst. Stepping forward towards the man he gently but firmly brought him to the front of the crowd:

"Now then my man, I want an honest answer to a straight-forward question," said he in a most professional no-nonsense manner, as he made the man throw down his fag-end. "How long have you had such a cough?"

The poor man appeared flustered and embarrassed and could only mutter that he didn't often cough, except on a morning on getting out of bed. The huge herbal man looked down upon the frail little man, sympathetically nodding his head in a wise fashion:

"Typical symptoms!" said he, his rich voice sounding a little despairing. "And you appear to have no voice at all. You sound, sir, like a mouse, and I don't say that unkindly or to raise a laugh. I am very serious. Unbutton your shirt..." Before the man could decide whether to comply or not, the quack doctor had assisted him in doing so, and taking up his stethoscope from the stall, he began sounding the man's chest: "Humph...take a deep breath sir, if you can, and another, humph..."

Finally, disengaging the stethoscope and placing it in his jacket pocket, he told the man to button up his shirt: "This morning cough of yours, it is a dry cough isn't it? A kind of choking cough and you have difficulty in bringing up phlegm haven't you?"

"Yes sir," replied the man looking surprised and nodding his head in acquiescence to every following remark! All the time the herbal man was questioning the man, he kept glancing knowingly and wisely round his audience as though signifying he had already diagnosed the man's malady (presuming he suffered from any other than malnutrition) and was now going to place him on the road to recovery. On the stall were test-tubes, mortars, an array of bottles of tablets and liquid medicines, and leaflets. Taking up one of the bottles of medicine, plus a leaflet he presented them to the small underfed man:

"Now then, do as I tell you: one tablespoon of this medicine to be taken at night before you go to bed, and repeat the dose on a morning when rising, and study the leaflet carefully."

The little man was obviously grateful and was certainly not a part of the quack's act. He nudged his way out of sight and no doubt was glad to do so! Young as I was, I was convinced that what the little man really required was a prescription, a permanent one, that could be dispensed freely at the butchers, the grocers, the fishmongers, the bakers, the fruiterers, the dairyman and the brewers!

There was no doubt that this isolated but heaven-sent incident was appearing to have some effect on some members of the audience, and when the black man appealed for anyone who might be a little hazy on their own state of health to step forward and consult him and rely upon his expert diagnosis, a number of them did just that. They took it in turns to approach him, and almost whispered to him what symptoms were troubling them; and he, though very critical of the medical profession and its ways, indulged in the same classical spot-check examinations which all of us usually associate with the trained medical fraternity. He peered into the patient's eyes, glanced at the tongue and the teeth, felt the pulse and sounded the chest, and of course appeared solemn and wise whilst doing so. A few leading questions accompanied every consultation, and as every hopeful client walked away clutching their purchased bottle of pills or medicine, the provider of such beneficence casually looked round at the rest of the lingering assembly, clearly admonishing them with his large and by now critical eyes: "Woe to all who do not seek my cures, for you alone shall be the losers in the long run!" One or two individuals shuffled nervously forward to consult him then purchase his wares, probably through a feeling of guilt or fear from the force of his accusing gaze. In his continuing remarks the herbal man was determined to express his contempt for the medical profession, especially for those individuals who had managed to build up and maintain a profitable private practice in such areas as London's Harley Street, which oddly enough coming from himself, he described as the "El-Dorado of the Charlatans"!

What attracted me to the next pitch, curiously enough, was the peculiarly strong aroma of liniment hanging over it. I was just in time to witness a middle-aged man being assisted by one of the stall-holders to strip to the waist, and to judge by his distorted countenance during the process, he appeared to be suffering acute discomfort in the upper part of his back. Another of the stall holders (and if I wasn't mistaken, the three of them were brothers) began rolling up his shirt sleeves as the pain-sufferer was being directed to place his hands on the stall and bend gently over. With apparent skill the masseur examined the man's back and shoulders, addressing the audience at the same time as he pointed to certain areas where the trouble was supposed to lie:

"Ladies and gentlemen, as you will have observed, this man is suffering a lot of pain, which is the result of an attack of acute fibrositis. Now, using my own special liniment, I am going to give him a thorough massage, and I want you all to observe carefully how I do this, for the massage is as important as the liniment! And indeed, this masseur who had given his lotion his own surname (Waugh's Liniment ,well-advertised through posters and on the bottle labels) spent quite some time on the massage, so determined was he to bring relief to this old boy. A con-merchant would have probably have spent no more than a couple of minutes demonstrating his supposed skills and the power of his lotion, then he would have got down to business of flogging the stuff.

After the treatment the man was able to dress himself unaided, and all the while he was pouring out his gratitude to his benefactor. Then it was time for the sales talk, and business was pretty brisk after he had waved around a number of written testimonials received from grateful clients. It took all three brothers to cope with the demand. The majority of those who purchased a bottle of liniment did not appear as though they were in need of it, and I reckoned they must have been purchasing it for someone else; either that, or they were hoping the very possession of it might act as a talisman against any approach of rheumatism.

From the moment I set eyes upon these three brothers, they reminded me of mountain climbers or rugby players. They certainly more resembled the athletic type then the makers of liniment. After their session had come to an end and the crowd dispersed, I lingered on, and I was pleased I did for I had my curiousity satisfied. After a few minutes the three of them stripped to the waist, and in a most unique manner, attracted their next crowd by beginning an amazing display of gymnastics the like of which could have not have been surpassed in any circus. Brother-number-one, the masseur, without showing any signs of strain whatever, balanced his brothers on his shoulders and arms, and slowly turned a complete circle. In no time at all they had another large audience round them. For five whole minutes they performed what were to my young mind almost impossible stunts! I began to think that if the application of Waugh's aromatic balm upon the body was solely responsible for such well developed men as these Waugh brothers, then it ought to be made available on free prescription for all those unable to afford it. Furthermore, Radio-Luxembourg ought to be advertising its merits non-stop, in place of devoting valuable Sunday listening time to such fictitious characters as 'Salty Sam and the Sailor Man'.

Leaving the Waugh brothers behind me, I stopped to listen for a few moments to Harry the Boot King. All the shipyard men and the factory workers patronised Harry, and it wasn't difficult to see why. One had only to look upon his fine, strong, handsome-looking wares to wish one was in work and able to afford such footgear.

The next character I came across was a most remarkable showman, and I don't claim this lightly, for already I had witnessed some outstanding performers. This man was known as the Human Ostrich! He was stripped to the waist, and though he was a light-weight, he possessed an extraordinary chest expansion, which was as well considering his act! He was just about to begin a fresh performance when I arrived on the scene. This started with him chewing and swallowing an electric light bulb. After partaking of this light delicacy, he strolled round his circle of onlookers distributing pieces of polished glass, marbles and small pebbles, then retracing his steps, he directed each recipient in turn to place the object they were holding into his mouth and with the aid of a sip of water he washed them down. Apparently not satisfied with this lot, he began swallowing a few razor blades, followed by a lit cigarette and the smoke from this was then ejected from his ears. Whenever he addressed his audience it was in a rather hoarse voice, and I was not surprised at this, considering the junk he was lowering down his gullet.

Like a lot of people, I was fully aware that we were living in hard times, and that grub of any description was difficult to come by without money, but I was nonetheless amazed as to how this chap was apparently seeking to overcome his problems by loading his stomach with such indigestible garbage. I could not imagine him ever being constipated for he was certainly getting more than his share of roughage in his diet. After lowering down his throat a pocket-watch and holding on to the end of the chain with his teeth, and recovering it again, he declared his intention of coming round with his cap to make a collection before performing his final act, which was to swallow a sword right to the hilt. As he came round, he enlightened us as to how he cleared the entrails of all the junk he swallowed during his performance: the drinking of seven or eight pints of Bass was the minimum required to flush it out! He depended on their generosity and he knew they would oblige; and they did. After the collection, he tilted his head back, sword in his right hand, and I witnessed what up to that moment I would have thought impossible! An Ostrich may be able to swallow as much scrap metal and other non-edible material as you like, but no Ostrich had ever to my knowledge, swallowed a sword. It amazed me the crazy things some people would do to earn a few shillings.

When I came across a stall full of novelties I was not in the least surprised at the size of the adult audience around it, nor at the enthusiasm being shown towards the tricks and games being exhibited by the chirpy stall-holder. I supposed that during hard times especially, some people are prone to seek out all forms of distraction in order to take their minds off their immediate discomforts. One particular trick, which appeared to command a lot of respect, was a currency-note-maker. A crisp slip of blank paper was placed into the compartment of this novelty, closed, then re-opened, and there was a freshly printed currency-note! The illusion was created because the toy consisted of a two-compartment box. In to one there is placed a genuine currency-note. I was a bit puzzled as to why so many hard up looking characters decided to invest in the purchase of one of those tricks, for to complete the illusion they would have to possess a real fresh, crisp pound or ten-shilling note; and I couldn't imagine any one of them having either of those, in any condition, long enough to play around with it. I felt sure there were one or two who were speculating on the novelty as a means of resolving their permanent state of insolvency, so taken in did they appear with the demonstration. Now I could see the wisdom of the two poorly-dressed men who each purchased a horrific face-mask. If by wearing the same they were to succeed into frightening out of their wits their immediate creditors, such as the landlord or ticket-man, their purchase would prove to be a sound investment.

A few feet away from the novelty stall was a restless creature pacing backwards and forwards over the same stretch of ground, with a kind of hunted-look upon his face. He was holding a pile of pamphlets under one arm, and accosting every passer-by, though to no avail:

"Get your *Old Moore's Almanack* here, at threepence a time. Read your horoscope and learn your future; only threepence a time."

Being as usual curious, I stood and observed his sales' progress, or rather lack of it; for no one was paying the least attention to him, apart from myself. Soon he was rewarding me with furtive glances; finally he approached me:

"Want to buy an *Old Moore's Almanack*, threepence?" he asked.

"You must be kiddin', Mister. Where would I get threepence from?"

He stared at me rather blankly for a few seconds as though unsure what to make of my response:

"You mean you've got nowt—then bugger off, don't stand starin' at me as though I was a freak or somethin'."

"I can stand where I like," I retorted, being a trifle annoyed at his remark.

"Not starin' at me you cannot. Nee bugger will buy me books with you standin' there starin' at me."

I sensed he was upset because no one was buying his books, so I wandered off towards another of the stalls which had a large crowd around it, wondering what they were staring at! The centre of attraction was a gipsy herbalist. On his stall were stacked two separate lots of small round boxes of the type that were commonly used by chemists for holding tablets, and ointment. There were also test tubes and a number of small bottles containing what looked suspiciously like samples of urine. Standing alongside the Gipsy, was a poorly dressed man who appeared to be thoroughly enjoying the attention that the herbalist was directing towards him. Taking up one of the small bottles from the stall, the herbalist held it up for all to observe:

"Ladies and gentlemen, this bottle contains a sample of this man's urine. Note the colour, and the sandy deposits in it, obvious signs of malfunction of the liver."

The shabbily-dressed man smiled as though he had just been paid a compliment by the Gipsy, instead of being informed by him publicly that his liver was out of order. The Gipsy continued in clear precise layman's terms, explaining the workings of the liver and the kidneys, and the main troubles that could upset the healthy functioning of those organs. Having instructed everyone present on this, he got straight down to business, which was to advertise his herbal tablets, which he claimed would not only remove all poison-charged fluids from the system, but would also assist in making the patient look and feel years younger. The gist of his message appeared to be: purchase the tablets and dose yourself with them whether your liver is upset or not. However, to impress anyone who may have been entertaining doubts about his claims as to what his herbal tablets were meant to do he gave a small demonstration which consisted of placing one of the herbal tablets into the bottle containing the smoky, sandy-looking urine sample. Within seconds the contents of the bottle became as clear as drinking water. This experiment definitely pleased the shabbily-dressed man, whose expression changed swiftly from surprise to gratitude, as though the action of the tablet in dissolving the sediments in his urine specimen had completely cured him of whatever malady he was supposed to be suffering from. It was when the Gipsy presented him with a free box of the tablets and dismissed him, that the poor man's countenance changed from that of pure simplicity and contentment, to that of gloom. It was obvious he was disappointed with his reward and most probably had been expecting or hoping for at least the price of a pint of beer.

When the Gipsy had satisfied every client who came forward to purchase his tablets, he began to draw attention to his herbal ointment, another natural product made by himself. The base of the ointment consisted of the fat of the hedgehog mixed into a paste with various healing herbs! As though at some pre-arranged and undetected signal, another shabbily-dressed individual shuffled forward towards the front of the stall, and sat on the stool provided for him and took off his shoes and socks. His shoes were not in too bad a state, but his socks were such that he would have been as well without them. It seemed as though all the local dossers were attending the Quayside that morning to have their various ailments attended to; not that anyone could find fault in that, for the poor chaps would be having continuous difficulty in finding the means to pay for their bed in some lodging house let alone afford a visit to a doctor. If this man's socks were in poor condition, rest assured his feet were also in a bad way, for apart from the usual deformities, which were probably the poverty-stricken legacy of a life-time of ill-fitting footwear, there were a number of prominent looking blisters on various parts of his feet. The Gipsy, employing a liberal amount of the green herbal ointment, gently massaged it all over the man's feet. Finally he told him to put his socks and shoes back on. The man complied, stood up, paced about a little, then triumphantly declared that he felt as though he had new feet. I reckoned he would certainly have sticky feet, and I could imagine those remants of stockings of his completely disintegrating when he attempted to remove them that night. After he had been presented with a box of ointment, and directed how to use it, this man, also appearing disappointed, returned to the crowd and stood next to the man who had been given the free tablets, with whom he was obviously acquainted.

Meanwhile, the Gipsy herbalist was not intending to rest the case for his ointment simply on the gratifying testimony of some hard-up dosser whose feet he had anointed with it. Far from it: it could be used for instance to cure dandruff, and also as a hairdressing; it would certainly plaster down the most unruly head of hair. It could also be used to combat and cure spots and pimples; and believe it or not, one could eat it, if one's tastes lay in that direction, with beneficial results especially for those prone to suffer from constipation. And to prove he was serious about being able to eat the ointment, he swallowed a portion of it. I observed the two dossers nearby, on witnessing the Gipsy taste the ointment with apparent relish, begin nodding wisely to one another as though agreeing. They would sample the ointment on their bread at tea time, and if no harmful effects were felt by late evening, they would also share out the tablets and have some with their supper. I supposed that after all, they would be accustomed to quaint dietary in the various lodging houses they frequented.

The next large crowd that attracted my interest, and which had just gathered on my arrival, was witnessing a shirtless man who was in the process of anointing his torso and arms with paraffin. After taking a swig of it, and spitting it out, he took hold of an iron rod which had a cloth secured to one end of it, and soaked it with the paraffin. He lit it, and began applying the torch to his body and arms and even into his mouth which resulted in him belching forth flames, not unlike an angry dragon. Blessed with my limited knowledge of the law of the land at that moment, I felt sure that his risking setting himself aflame must surely constitute an offence even though the person concerned would almost certainly be a registered unemployed man, and his self-incineration would save the Public Treasury the sum of fifteen shillings unemployment benefit every week! On the ground, in the middle of the ring, lay lengths of rope, chain, a medieval strait-jacket, and a couple of swords resting on top of his shirt and coat. I was completely mystified as to what he intended doing with that lot. Even when he mentioned that he was a pupil of the great Houdini, the escapologist, I remained none the wiser.

Extinguishing the torch and placing it on the ground he picked up the strait-jacket, and in a very hoarse voice, no doubt aggravated by singeing his throat, he appealed to any sport in the crowd to volunteer to secure him up. For a while it did not seem that anyone was willing to step forward to assist him thereby satisfying my curiosity. Then a Sailor, who was being tempted to show off by his girl-friend, came forward. Following instructions he began by first placing the showman into the strait-jacket, and to judge by the way the Sailor went to work in securing him into this tortuous contraption, he was enjoying the opportunity of showing off in front of his girl-friend and the crowd in general. If the poor man had not been secured by any other means than the strait-jacket, I would have sworn that his task of releasing himself would be almost impossible.

But the jacket was only the beginning of his problem; lengths of rope and chain followed and for this Sailor required no instruction. He was apparently an expert when it came to tying-up. He soon had the exhausted-looking man appearing like a trussed-up corpse ready for burying at sea; one sword prised down in between the bindings back and front, completed the task! I had up to that moment imagined that all possible odd characters existed in my own neighbourhood and I included myself among the numbers, but this particular Sunday morning visit to the Quayside was an eye-opener. That anyone should allow such torment upon themselves for a mere pittance was to me eccentricity of the highest order. The Sailor picked up the man's cap from the ground, placed it between the showman's teeth and guided him around the audience. Afterwards the Sailor totted up the proceeds: just over four shillings from such a large gathering. Before making any attempt to escape from his bonds, he appealed for a number of sports to throw in a few more coppers to bring the sum up to five shillings. But it appeared the getting of those extra pennies was going to be the hardest part of the act; the odd pennies were slow in coming in. Finally the Sailor dropped the remaining sixpence in the kitty himself to make the five bob up. Although it took the escapeologist only a few minutes to free himself, I reckoned he put in as much effort and lost as much sweat as a navvy would in digging out a pipe-channel non-stop for an hour. I was relieved to leave his presence for I felt as tortured as he must have been.

Now every kid in my neighbourhood knew something about horse-racing, indeed it would have been practically impossible not to be acquainted with this sport of kings for quite a number of the bookmakers occupied a wash-house in someone's backyard for his office in return for a small fee. Most of us kids at various times would overhear our fathers audibly yearning for that other horse to get first past the post in order to clinch the double, and so be able to afford a night out on the terrace. It was the dream of every street-corner man to get that threepenny or sixpenny treble up, and that all popular newspaper the *Sporting Man*, would change hands between them as regularly as their betting fancies did. Therefore I had been confident, having in mind the patter of the street-corner experts, how I expected racing tipsters to appear, to talk, and to perform! But I was completely dismayed when I came across the first tipster, a shabby-looking character who was desperately attempting to make out he was a spiv. As regarding his horse-talk, he couldn't have had a clue as to what he was talking about, and the majority of his audience was making fun of him. He didn't appear to sense this, or else he was putting a brave face on it. To judge by his answers to the questions he was being asked, he had probably never set foot upon a racecourse in his life; and if he had had any close acquaintance with horse-flesh, it must have been whenever he opened a tin of corned beef. The majority of his congregation were laughing at every comment he made, and they laughed all the more when three or four individuals stepped forward and purchased his tips, at threepence a time. It was quite possible from what I could gather from some of the men in the crowd confiding in each other,

*'One-eyed Scotty', a racing tipster on the Quayside, 1905*

that this poor fellow, after a period of observing two or three professional tipsters on the Quayside, had concluded (wrongly in his case) that anyone could get in on the act, and make a few shillings without any apparent outlay whatever.

The next tipster, who was situated about twenty yards away, was a different bet altogether: a military-looking gentleman, addressing himself as Captain Kiwi. After listening to this man for about fifteen minutes, I sensed that if it was possible to tip positive horse-winners, then surely he was the one to do so; he appeared to know the horse-racing world absolutely, and without relying upon the *Sporting Man* or any other racing chronicles, which he made fun of. And his memory was equal to his task; he could roll off his tongue the names of all the favourite horses, jockeys, trainers and others, whom he had tipped successfully the previous month. Furthermore, he was a good actor, and undoubtedly a good psychologist, able to weigh up most of his audience. He casually let out that he was on regular drinking and dining terms with Peers of the Realm, and their trainers; and no doubt to reinforce his extravagant claims, he brought from his back trouser-pocket a wad of pound notes that made most of his audience gasp with envy. As he carelessly fondled the notes, he peered round the crowd meaningfully, before continuing:

"Tomorrow, I'll be at Nottingham races; meeting up with some old friends, jockeys and owners; and of course backing a few winners. It is entirely up to anyone here this morning to decide whether they wish to share in my luck. You all know my reputation, I don't push you, you make your own mind up. Captain Kiwi is not short of a pound or two. But whenever I have any good information, I like to share it with my friends, many of whom I note are in my audience this morning."

Surprisingly enough, only a few individuals in his large audience saw fit to display any signs of mirth or scorn at his wondrous claims. It was his commanding address and sheer force of personality that won him the day as far as the majority were concerned; and his information, presented in sealed envelopes was in great demand. My opinion of him from the beginning, was that he earned his fees solely for his entertainment value! Mind you there were flaws in his make-up; some of his remarks could only be suspect after a close critical observation of his dress. I won't deny that for the depressed 1930s he was presentable in his threadworn genteel-looking suit, and well polished dut. But one would have thought he could well do with another suit for Sunday use, and surely he would not have missed three pounds off that thick roll of banknotes; assuming they were genuine.

On leaving the racing Captain behind me, I caught sight of Davie! He was the Saturday afternoon matinée crier, employed by the local cinema in Benwell, the Grand. It was his job to entice all the approaching matinée kids into the Grand if he observed that we were displaying the least inclination towards the Majestic Cinema (situated on the opposite side of the road). Davie was busy hawking small items like bootlaces, safety pins and needles and thread. One of the most conspicuous points about him, was his feet, classic Chaplin in size shape and gait; all he required was a dut and walking stick and he would have appeared to all the world as the master clown himself! Knowing him well, I approached him and spoke:

"Hello, Davie. Are you makin' much?"

His eyes lit up in a show of annoyance; it didn't take too much to upset him at any time:

"No I am not. Nee bugger's buyin' owt off me. My stuff's not good enough for them, they would sooner buy the swag off the stalls..."

Davie was not one to address himself solely to a particular individual when he was really after rebuking everyone in sight whom he felt were doing him down:

"See if I care if they don't want any bloody laces or safety pins." This last remark was directed especially for the benefit of a young couple who were strolling by at that moment and who were obviously giggling at Davie's display of annoyance: "Giggle away you buggers, I'll bet you can't afford laces or pins." This only increased their mirth; and my tactlessness at the time did nothing to ease his temper:

"They're just laughin' at you Davie, I wouldn't be bothered with them if I were you." He shuffled round to face me as swiftly as those large feet of his would allow him to and was on the point of paying me off for my helpful comment, when suddenly a couple of lads a little older than myself, called out to him:

"Davie! You're not supposed to fiddle when you're being kept by the Parish."

His first reaction was to swiftly conceal the small cardboard box containing his wares beneath his jacket; then on reflection he brought it out again and turned to face his tormentors:

"Go on, bugger off the pair of you cheeky wasters, nee Parish keeps me, I work for my coppers, that's more than your old man does. Tell him that if you like."

"You're a liar, Davie," called out the second lad. "I've seen the Means Test man at your door many a time, so there. You're kept for nowt by the Parish..."

Davie made towards them in a threatening manner, not that he would have an earthly chance of catching hold of them: "I'll put my boot up yeh backsides, go on, bugger off an' leave me alone."

I thought it was time I made myself scarce, in case he returned and blamed me for all his troubles. Looking over to the other side of the river up to the church clock, I learned it was twelve-fifty p.m. It was time I made for home or else all the Yorkshire Pudding would be devoured in my absence. Deciding to leave the Quayside by another route, I began climbing the Castle Garth Stairs, and I was surprised to learn there were a number of small shops situated on such an out-of-the-way location. There was a barber's shop, a secondhand shop, and a boot shop which was open; an old lady was standing at the shop door:

*Castle Garth Stairs, 1931*

"Hello missis. There's plenty of stairs aboot here," I remarked.

"Hello, son. Been on the Quayside have you?"

"Yes missis. An' there's some comical people down there," I replied.

She smiled: "You can say that again, hinny. Going home for your dinner now?"

"Yes Missis. I hope yeh sell all your boots when the people come up here from the Quayside; that's if they don't buy them off Harry the Boot King. Ta ta."

I climbed back on to my imaginary horse and set off at a gallop. Just as I was about to pass by the Rifle public house on Scotswood Road, out came my Uncle Charley. He was married to my Aunt Dolly, whose secondhand shop I observed was open:

"Hello Uncle Charley. Are you gannin' home for your dinner?" I inquired. He took out his pocket-watch, as though to reassure himself that it was not pub-closing time:

"No of course not, the pubs don't close until two o'clock, you know that," said he, as though implying I frequented them often enough. "Where have you been?"

"The Quayside, Uncle. But divint tell anyone; I'm not supposed to gan that far. If me dad gets t'know I'll get me bait put up."

"Here's a penny, catch the tram, and don't say I never give you anything." And off he hurried to his next pub of call, only a few yards away. There was no danger of me spending money on tramfare. I was about to cross over to my own side of the road and without bothering to look to my right, when I suddenly heard the screeching of cycle brakes being applied, turning swiftly I realised I had nearly stepped into the path of one of Tom Wall's 'Stop Me and Buy One!' Ice-cream cycle carriers.

"Can't yeh leuk where yeh gannin', yeh little bugger?" remonstrated the salesman.

"Why don't you sound your bell like the tramcar drivers do?" I asked. He was about to vent further his rising temper, when I remembered the penny my Uncle had given me. "Anyway, it's just as well you pulled up, Mister, 'cause I want a penny ice." His attitude changed instantly:

"What flavour do yeh want, son. Lemon or Orange?"

"Orange please." And so we left each other, at peace with the world!

# The Lamplighter

One winter's night on leaving a building site after having scrounged some firewood from the night watchmen, I was suddenly accosted by a man who begged me to act as his look-out while he climbed up a particular lamp-post in a back lane, in order to nick the gas-mantle. He claimed he couldn't afford to buy one, and that his kids were sitting in the dark at home. I appreciated how he must have felt, having been after firewood, and if the watchman had been absent I'm afraid I too would have helped myself. So I stood at the corner of the lane acting as his scout while he accomplished his task in safety! Mind you, whether that public gas-mantle he nicked would have fitted his own gas fitting at home I didn't know, but I hoped it would, for I knew by experience what it was like to sit in the dark due to not having the coppers to buy a mantle or for any other reason!

I reckoned the resulting trouble created for the lamplighter next day, would be slight when compared to the regular mishandling of the street-lamps at the hands of the younger fraternity. Some of the lads in my district, when they were not using their catapult in order to take pot-shots at tin cans, dustbins, or someone's cat, practised their skill by directing their missiles towards the street-lamps, shattering the glass panes and also putting paid to the gas-mantles. Then there were other acts of sabotage, more mild in effect than the misuse of catapults, but still guaranteed to creat problems for the lamplighter. When the young lasses hitched their ropes onto the arms of the lamps in order to make their own maypole, their continuous swinging round the lamps often shattered the mantles, and also, I believe, interfered with the lamps' clockwork!

It was at school that I learned from one of the teachers that songs and poetry had been composed about the public lamplighter; and I reckoned he was worthy of such romantic recognition, for in the minds of most of us we appreciated that he brought us light, and made us feel secure as we wandered abroad in the long dark nights of winter! However, I did witness on a number of occasions, a few courting couples who obviously did not

*Lamplighter on the Swing Bridge*

look upon the lamplighter in such a romantic vein, for on entering the back lane, the young man would ascend the lamp-post and calmly turn off the gaslight as though he was in his own bedroom. This act of sabotage or convenience, as no doubt lovers would term it, was not only a problem to the lamplighter, but also to the regular backlane traffic which was brisk as a great number of families used their back doors more often than they did their front entrance on account of the front room in many instances having to serve as a bedroom. The first time I ever remember setting eyes upon my local lamplighter was when I was five years old and in the company of my elder sister, on the way to the fish and chip shop. I stood engrossed in his activities, while my sister was in the shop waiting her turn to be served. His tools of trade, I learned later from him in person, were practically identical to those of the early lamplighters. A short ladder, equipped with hooks on the top of it for resting on the arms or shoulders of the lamp-post, a pole, which had a lug on it for opening the lamp window, and a lantern, from which he could transfer a flame to the burners after turning on the gas supply. The main difference in relation to my local lamplighter from that of his earlier counterpart, was in his possessing a cycle, which he rode to cover his fair-sized round.

Before becoming acquainted with our local lamplighter, I had in my innocence assumed that all he did was to cycle round his district in the morning, checking to see all street-lamps were properly extinguished, and returning at dusk to ensure they were all in service. I was surprised to learn of the various tasks he had to perform; practically the whole maintainence of the lamps on his round were carried out by him: replacing damaged gas mantles, and the lamp's windows had to be cleaned and also replaced if broken, then the lamp clocks which controlled the distribution of gas to the lamps had to be wound up; and there were other little jobs to attend to. Apart from his midday lunch break he was kept busy from the time he set off on his round on a morning until he finished in the evening; and he still found time to have a few words with such as myself, or anyone who showed an interest in his work.

Time sounded the death-knell of the old lamplighter; and another age-old friend retired from the scene and into the memory closet of all those who wished to harbour him!

# The Blacksmith

There were two blacksmiths' shops in my locality, one, at the bottom of the lane, and the other situated on the quarry behind the Grand Cinema. Naturally the first one I became acquainted with was the one down the lane; it was the musical sound of the hammer striking the anvil that attracted me and drew me towards the entrance to the workshop. I stood entranced at the near-magical experience, observing the comforting glow of the forge fire, the smell of burnt hoof, and the smithy, tongs in hand, supporting the white-hot iron shoe which he was about to place on the anvil. Then he began beating it to the required shape and thickness. But before he had gained this objective, the horseshoe had lost most of its heat, so once more he placed it into the coals of the forge fire and began working the enormous bellows with his right foot until the fine coal-slack turned a bright

*Blacksmiths at work in Benwell, possibly at Thirlwell Cottages*

red, then to all the colours of the rainbow, and eventually to a gleaming white heat. Retrieving the glowing white horseshoe from the forge with his tongs, and after a little more beating into shape, he swiftly turned about, raised the horse's rear left hoof up between his leather aproned thighs and planted the hot iron shoe firmly onto the hoof. Then to my amazement he began securing it by means of knocking nails into the hoof! Being then ignorant of the horse's anatomy, I wondered whether it suffered as a result of being fitted up with new shoes; and if it did, why not raise its opposite free leg and send its tormentor to meet, head on, the nearby stone wall. Time he got busy on the hoof with the large rasp filing in order to create a smooth finish, I gazed around his workshop: the forge appeared to occupy the whole of the centre of the shop, and all his work tools not in use at that moment were suspended from the front of it by means of hooks and bars. His anvil, situated near the forge, was mounted on a huge unshaped block of wood, a good part of which was buried in the floor to make it secure.

One of the main characteristics of this man, the first blacksmith I had seen, I discovered the moment he glanced up from his work to bestow a greeting upon me. This was his genuine warmth and gentle friendship, hallmarks of a man contented with his work and life in general. From then on I made regular visits and passed many a while watching him work, often speculating as to what trade the horse he was shoeing at that particular moment was engaged in: for instance did it haul the local ice-cream cart? Or fishcart? Was it in the coal trade? Furniture? Bakery? The rag trade? Or tea delivery? Through time and experience I was able to distinguish between the often forlorn creature of the hawker, and those of the undertakers, bakers and tea merchants, for the latter-mentioned beasts were often taller, certainly more graceful, well-groomed and well-fed, and always appeared contented. Indeed they more resembled race-horses than day-to-day work beasts on the city streets. One could sense they were getting their fair quota of oats, apart from all the other necessary attention that goes to make a horse's life a happy one.

Mind you, I was not the only individual who whiled time away just inside the smithy's shop observing the work in progress. One particular old gaffer would surely be there, sitting on some make-shift seat kindly provided by the smith, smoking his old clay-pipe and spitting out excess saliva; much to my disgust. However, some of his yarns were entertaining and worth listening to first time round: perhaps on the follies of the Boer War, and the First World War. Through time, not only myself, but the blacksmith, closed our ears to the monotonous repetition of his tales which became more exaggerated the more he told them; I felt sure even the horses yawned through sheer boredom. Thankfully, the old gaffer obviously preferred a silent audience. So when the blacksmith and I ceased to pass any comment about his continuously repeated exploits, he no doubt assumed our interest in his chatter was too intent to bother him with any form of questioning.

One day whilst playing in the lane, one of the neighbours asked me to oblige her by taking her stock-pot down to the blacksmith to have the handle welded back on. Time I waited, he fixed it, and charged threepence:

"Tell your mother, nipper, I've welded that handle so well, it won't ever break again," said he.

"It's not for my mother," said I, being rather exact about it.

"It doesn't matter who it's for does it? Tell her I've made a good job of it."

Naturally I thought the smithy had repaired the pot-handle as a token of good-will; but later on I witnessed him making a set of quoits for a miner. This set me to thinking that the blacksmith possessed other skills than simply shoeing horses; so I questioned him. He pointed to the old gaffer sitting in the doorway filling his pipe with strong Rubicon Twist:

"Ask Toby there. He used to be a blacksmith in the army."

The old gaffer lit up, and after the air had cleared and his pipe was glowing satisfactorily, he urged me to sit down and make myself comfortable as though intending to take a week over his tale:

"Well son. It has long been the custom of the local smith to repair the housewife's pots and pans and kettles, providing of course he has spare time on his hands, for you understand, the welfare of the horse has to remain his first priority, it did in my time..."

"There's still plenty of horses around, Toby, to keep me busy," interjected the active blacksmith.

Toby ignored this comment, and instead asked me whether I could recall the Tinker that used to come around the lanes and repair all the pots and pans?

"When was that Mister?" I asked.

Toby took a deep pull on his pipe, scratched his head, then asked me how old I was. "I'm ten, mister."

He peered at me intently as though I was after playing games with him:

"You're only ten! Then you wouldn't remember the old Tinker that used to come around Benwell; it's over twenty years since he was last round! Now then, when I was in the army (I was in the Boer War, you know; cavalry regiment) men in my trade were kept busy morning till night; the army couldn't do without the blacksmith in those days; they're not so much wanted these days, they've got tanks..."

*Blacksmith's shop in Cullercoats, 1899*

"They've still got horses in the army today Toby," called out the working blacksmith. But it appeared that Toby was intent on ignoring his friend. I don't think he liked any form of opposition whenever he was talking.

"The smithy, my lad, is one of the oldest trades going. You ought to have learned that fact at school; I never went to school; when I was your age, my father put me straight to work in my Uncle's blacksmith's shop to learn the trade. By the time I was twenty, son, I not only could shoe a horse well, but I could make, and repair, any piece of farming equipment you care to mention. My uncle taught me every trick of the trade; including how to smoke a pipe, ha ha ha! Not only did we make pots and pans in our spare time, but garden gates that were a wonder to look at; for the posh people living in the big houses; gentry I suppose. Yes Laddie, the smithy, is the salt of the earth!"

As Toby continued, I was not surprised to learn that in days of yore the smith's skills were not entirely devoted to peaceful pursuits. He was kept busy by forging and repairing swords and lances, for the King and his followers, the Knights and Barons; and when gunpowder was invented, he very soon adapted his skills to the making and repairing of muskets and pistols. His services would also be called upon in the Castle dungeon, to break off the shackles from some prisoner who was about to be released, or executed!

One day, on my way home from school, I witnessed a coal-merchant's horse slip and fall outside the Adelaide Cinema on the terrace. Even when the poor creature was released from its cart, it still took a number of onlookers, including the local Policeman on the beat, a few more minutes to get it back on to its feet; and the remarks of the Bobby to the coal-merchant, that his horse required shoeing, remained impressed on my mind. Of course the coalman retorted bluntly that he couldn't afford to have his horse newly shod. But the Policeman equally bluntly told him further that he couldn't afford not to shoe his horse, reminding him that the next time the poor beast may not be so fortunate in escaping serious injury!

On seeing Toby, later, I remarked to him about the accident:

"The Bobby, was right, laddie. Every town horse that is trudging up and down cobbled streets and lanes six days a week, ought to be re-shod every 250 miles of travelling!"

I reckoned the poor horses of most of the hawkers, were in the same predicament as myself and were only re-shod when their shoes fell apart.

# Jubilee Day 1935

On Jubilee Day, Monday 6th May, I was up early as usual, for although we kids had a day's holiday from school, I still had my newspapers to deliver. After eating my ration of bread and drinking my weak tea, I left the house by the back way, because I wanted to see how far the lane committee had progressed with the decorations. I was pleased to learn they hadn't finished the job, so I hoped by the time I returned from the newsagents I might get the opportunity to decorate the lamp-post outside our back door, for I had volunteered my services the previous night. On my way I thought eagerly of the afternoon tea party that was to be held in the backlane to celebrate the Jubilee of King George V and Queen Mary: twenty-five years they had been on the throne. What a long time to hold a job down, thought I. Their Insurance Cards would be well stamped-up!

On the previous Friday afternoon before we broke up from school for the long weekend, everyone in our class had been given a tin of toffees; on the lid were stamped the portraits of the King and Queen. The toffees were all gone but I had given the tin to my mother to keep buttons in; that would ensure it was preserved for years to come.

My gaffer was loading my bag with the papers when I entered the shop: "Hello Tich, son. You're the first here as usual. Now then, you'll find your bag is a little heavier this morning, because the *Journal* has a supplement. It's a special edition, Tich, on account of the Jubilee. But I can rely on you, son."

I slung the bag over my well-developed shoulders and instantly felt the difference in weight: I felt he ought to have asked me whether I could also support the extra weight of a large bacon sandwich. Instead he remarked:

"By the way Tich. There's sure to be a demand for the *Journal* this morning so I've put six copies in your bag for sale, so use your vocal cords, son, and try and get rid of them."

He was another of those characters who mistook me for a miniature cart-horse! However, I managed to sell four of them by the end of my round. On my way back to the shop I sat down on a garden wall and feasted myself on a chunk of cake supplied to me by a very observant lady who undoubtedly had realised I was in need of it. At the same time, I glanced through one of the remaining *Journals*; it was full of the impending celebrations about to take place all over the country, including pages of photographs portraying scenes from the accession to the throne, right up to the present time. One photo that attracted my special interest was King George, stooping to converse with a young pit lad, for the nipper resembled me, in almost every detail: his size, good looks and shabby clothes.

Well, thought I, it proves he's not stuck up. So if he happened to cross my path any time, I wouldn't feel embarrassed. I read also that the Lord Mayor of Newcastle was to take the salute at a march-by of Servicemen and Territorials on the Town Moor, at ten-thirty, that morning. I learned that messages and telegrams were flowing into Buckingham Palace from all quarters; even one congratulatory telegram from an unemployed man, living in George Street, who had received one from the King in return! I hoped, for his sake, that the Dole Office did not identify him, for sure enough, the Means-Test Man would be after enquiring of him as to how he could afford to send telegrams. There was also a telegram from Hitler! Being a newsboy who regularly read the papers I delivered, I was well informed on the goings-on of such characters, and I read the text of his message out of curiosity:

"I beg your Majesty to accept my sincerest congratulations and those of my Government on the 25th anniversary of your Majesty's accession to the Throne, and the best wishes for your Majesty's and her Majesty's personal well-being. The German people follow with hearty sympathy all efforts of your Majesty and the Royal British Government for strengthening peace, and hope that these efforts may be successful for the welfare of the British Empire and be a blessing for the whole world!"

Another item of news that caught my discerning eye, was that all able-bodied recipients of Parish relief would get an extra 1*s*. 6*d* for the occasion. Well, it was a hand-out not to be sniffed at: the price of a good feed in the Lockhart's Café, or three pints of Bass. I felt sure that if the Parish were going to give a treat to the outdoor recipients, then those recipients residing in the Workhouse, would be sure to be getting a bit extra today; without having to ask for it, like little Oliver Twist!

On my way home, I resisted the temptation to linger at the head of any of

*George V Silver Jubilee decorations in Northumberland Street, 1935*

the local lanes or streets to observe the feverish activities of their Jubilee decorators with their paint-pots, chalks, flags and buntings. I was in too much of a hurry to get back to my own pitch; when it came to such things as public tea-parties, there was no one more patriotic than myself, and also I was most desirous to offer my services in any manner to hasten the preparations. Walking down our lane, I was surprised to witness Mr Harris, usually one of the most aloof of men, up on top of a ladder busy decorating a lamp post with bunting; incidentally, the lamp I had volunteered to do. Nearby was Mr Fender, artistically drawing a large Union Jack on his back door with the use of appropriately coloured chalks. Indeed, I observed a number of individuals employed in the same manner, due no doubt to the lack of real flags; what few there were of those were hoisted on the top of wireless masts, and clothes-props secured to door-lintels. Mr Fender, happening to look up and away from his own particular chore and on to that of Mr Harris, up on the ladder with an armful of bunting, suddenly called out:

"Dick, hinny! You've got your colours mixed up. You should have red, white, then blue, in that order." And he pointed towards his back door where it could be seen that his masterpiece was nearly complete. "See what I mean, Dick, hinny? Red, white, then blue, what does it mean to you?" And he grinned wisely.

"Who's doing this job, Matty, yee or me?" retorted Dick, sounding none too pleased at being made conspicuous.

"I divint mean any harm, Dick, hinny," replied Mr Fender, pacifyingly; which might have closed the issue, except that Mrs Bell, living up to her usual character, interjected:

"Matty's reet, we've got to leuk our best, Mr Harris, so git the colours reet, hinny." Down the ladder came Mr Harris, leaving the rest of the bunting slung over the arms of the lamp:

"Bugger the Jubilee, I've had enough. I'll go and get meself dressed and dee my celebrations on Scotswood Road in the Hydraulic."

And off he went into his backyard, clashing the back door behind him. "What's come over with him, Daisy?" remarked Mr Fender, appearing surprised.

"Well, you've upset him; you should have kept quiet. You know he's a man who keeps to himself," replied Mrs Bell, ignoring her own interference.

"I was only trying to be helpful," said Matty, now looking dejected.

"Now we need someone to finish the lamp-post," replied Daisy.

"I'll do it, Mrs Bell," said I.

She peered at me critically: "Will you be able to manage up a ladder?" she asked.

"I can climb trees in the park, four times as high as any lamp-post; and I'll get the colours reet," I remarked eagerly. And without waiting for her to express further doubts, I was up the ladder in a flash. I observed one of my brothers run into the house, and I sensed his mission. I was busy placing the bunting colours in their proper order, when I heard the brisk command of my father:

"Tom! Come down that ladder, I want no accidents in my family."

I descended and sat down on the doorstep as he went back indoors.

"Grown-ups, they maak me sick," I muttered; and I cursed my brother who had snitched on me. It seemed that almost everyone was intent on preventing me getting up in the world! Mr Fender, glancing over at me as though I was a fellow-sufferer in misfortune, approached me:

"You saw what happened, Tommy. I didn't upset Mr Harris; I only remarked about the colours being mixed up! You see, I've heard that the Lord Mayor may be coming, an' we want to look our best."

Ensuring that Mrs Bell was well out of earshot, I remarked: "I think it was Mrs Bell, who upset him."

This suggestion appeared to appease him.

"That's it, Tommy, son. He cannot stan' women bossin' him aboot."

Now that the lane was a mass of decorations and the work of it completed, they began bringing out the tables and forms from the backyards where they had been stored since Saturday. Goodness knows where the trestle tables and forms came from; no one in the lane owned them. I began sounding out the kids up my end of the lane: some of them believed they were on loan from the nearby Salvation Army hall on Buddle Road. Others opted for the Mission next door to the Army, while a few declared they were from the Presbyterian Chapel, situated at the top of the street near the Sutton Dwellings. But I placed no faith in any of the suppositions. Considering those three named religious houses catered for every street in the district, all of whom were also holding Jubilee parties, none of the three churches could be seen to be favouring one particular street-party in preference to another. So I finally asked Mr Fender, who was busy putting the finishing touches to his Union Jack on his back door; he would be bound to know—considering he had remarked to me that the Lord Mayor was probably paying us a visit in the afternoon.

"The tables an' forms, son? I reckon the Board of Guardians must have supplied them," said he.

After that remark, I decided to give him up as hopeless.

By now the committee were placing tablecloths on the tables; which I thought was unusual or foolhardy, for we kids were to have the first sitting; well it was their look-out. I observed Mrs Simpson and Mrs Stephenson enter the lane, an arm apiece around Granny Newton. Following behind them came Mr Simpson carrying her wickerwork armchair, Mr Stephenson with the cracket and cushion for to rest her feet upon, and in the rear, Mrs Miller holding a remarkably huge shawl. Granny Newton had been confined to bed for a few weeks during the previous winter, with rheumatism. All the Jubilee team nearby, men, women and the older girls, ceased what they were doing for a few moments to greet and fuss over her; and the dear old soul appeared both pleased and dignified about it. Goodness knows how old she was, for whenever anyone asked her, she usually added or deducted two or three years from the previous age she had admitted to. It was generally agreed she was aged between 80 and 90 years. Her Victorian mode of dress reminded me of Old Mother Riley, of cinema-screen fame. Her dark bonnet secured under her chin, long dark skirt, dark blouse buttoned up to the throat, and ankle-length boots buttoned up the sides, completed the picture.

Standing at the next back door down the lane from Granny Newton's was old Mr Hardy, dressed in dark trousers and braces, a striped flannel shirt with a knotted scarf round his neck in place of collar and tie, and unlaced boots. He began fondling his abundant white moustache and critically observing the full attention that Granny Newton was receiving and enjoying; he was probably ruminating on a particular Saturday night in March, when he was nearly knocked down by a tramcar on Scotswood Road, and had to be assisted home in a state of shock by a Policeman. And the only commiseration he had received from any of the neighbours was to look where he was going after coming out of the pub! Suddenly, young Willie Carr, who was in my class at school, and possessed vocal powers that no town-crier could equal cried out:

"There's a ginger cat! Leuk, on the waal, it's tryin' t'pull doon the decorations, leuk at it everybody!" All action ceased and pandemonium almost broke out. It had been agreed the day beforehand that anyone who had cats or a dog would keep them indoors on this particular occasion; except for allowing them out for a few minutes in the front street which was quiet and deserted.

"It leuks like the cat that belangs to Mr Douglas," cried out Mrs Bell. Unbeknownst to her, Mr Douglas, a tall gaunt wiry-looking man, had just appeared on his back doorstep:

"That's noo my cat. Think again, Mrs Bell." There was an ominous sound in his swift denial of ownership of the rebel cat, and Daisy looked hastily around her immediate surroundings as though seeking someone she could attach blame to for her own indiscretion. For a brief moment I thought she intended once again to pass the buck on to Mr Fender, but she resisted the temptation:

"Of course it's not your cat, hinny; yours is a bigger one than that," declared Daisy.

Meanwhile, Mr Greenwood, who appeared to be practicing the art of snooker using a clothes-prop for a cue, finally dislodged the cat; it sprang off the wall on to one of the tables, and then the poor creature was chased out of sight by a crowd of joy-seeking kids; and in turn they were instantly rebuked by an angry-looking Mr Douglas!

I observed a number of the lane-committee were forming a group, with Granny Newton in the middle of them, to have their photo taken by Mr Wallace; Mr Fender, who was now occupied blowing-up balloons, was steadfastly refusing to join in. All of the women had taken off their white aprons for the occasion, no doubt to show off their best frocks which they were wearing that day, and the men with the exception of Mr Hardy, who had been invited to join in, had all put on their jackets and appeared spick-and-span. Mr Hardy, standing directly behind his wife and seemingly scowling down upon her as a result of a critical remark she had just made to him, was still in his shirt sleeves and braces. Despite appeals from the whole company, added to that of his wife, he was refusing to go indoors and put on his jacket:

"I'm either geud enough as I am or else taak the picture withoot me, I'm content either way," he bluntly remarked.

Mr Addison, standing alongside on the left of Mr Hardy, and dressed in his Sunday suit plus a new hard-hat and jewelled tiepin, resembled a prosperous pawnbroker rather than the window-cleaner that he was by profession; and he could not wholly conceal his contempt for his near neighbour, giving that coatless individual grim side-glances. Coming to a hasty decision, he discreetly moved himself on to the semi-circular group, and smiled with relief.

"Now then, all together, give me a big smile," called out Mr Wallace. Mrs Bell and Mrs Hardy did their best to oblige.

"Come on Mr Hardy, give me a smile," urged Mr Wallace, wearily.

"Get on with it, man, for goodness sake," retorted Mr Hardy, who then bared his teeth in the same fashion as his wife and Mrs Bell.

After a couple of shots, the photographer took snaps of those children who volunteered; for, surprisingly enough, quite a number of them, including myself, refused to have anything to do with what we took as some form of regimentation; we got enough of that business at school and at home. But my two sisters obliged and saved the family honour.

Once more the committee women and the older girls donned their aprons, and got busy laying the tables ready for the first sitting. At that moment Mrs Fender came out into the lane and began relating some news she'd heard on her Rediffusion wireless set. Part of the spectators' staging on the Town Moor had collapsed just as the Lord Mayor was about to take the salute! Most of the casualties were schoolboys; and all the injured had been taken to the Infirmary. Her husband had ceased working with the balloons in order to pay attention to the news bulletin, then remarked dismally:

"The Lord Mayor, won't turn up now, not now, not after that accident."

"It's the bairns I'm more concerned aboot, not whether the Lord Mayor's coming here or not," replied his wife reprovingly. But her tone had no effect on her husband who had returned his attention once more to the blowing up of balloons:

"That's all you're fit for," muttered his wife angrily, "getting rid of wind." And she went back indoors without making any visible impression upon her husband's composure.

The backlane was now crowded to saturation point; new babies accompanied by new mothers and fathers, not-so-new parents, middle-aged parents, grannies and grandads, in-laws, uncles and aunts, toddlers finding their feet, juniors, seniors, and those kids who had left school but were unemployed! The moment we kids had been waiting for had arrived, and all the elders had congregated to witness the tables being loaded with the Jubilee harvest and thrill at the sight of us kids paying our respects to it in the only possible way! From the backyard of Mrs Burns, which had been detailed as the supply base and kitchen, came an endless stream of white aprons, the wearers holding in each hand a large plate loaded with various sandwiches, chunks of stotty-cake with meat paste, sausage rolls, sly cakes, Russian cakes, currant buns and fancy cakes of every description. And all of us onlookers stood with our backs to the walls to leave a clear path to the tables. This task completed, Mrs Bainbridge, heading the team of Marshals, detailed all of us to our respective places at the tables. Before the tea was poured out, Mrs Bainbridge in a perfectly musical treble voice and in the manner of a trained Sunday School instructor, had us say grace:

"We thank God our maker, for what we are about to receive. And bless our King and Queen. A-men."

virtues which the believers themselves ought to be manifesting! It was at such times that I was reminded of the remark my father once made to a friend of his, when they were discussing the origin of Man: "No one calling himself a wise God would be foolish enough to create the human race!"

However, my mother believed in God, and her word and faith were good enough for me.

**************

The characters and scenes related above, are gone forever; yet they express an era that was as real and as vital as any past period in our social history.